CONFUCIAN REFLECTIONS

Confucian Reflections: Ancient Wisdom for Modern Times is about the early Chinese Confucian classic the *Analects* (*Lunyu* 論語) attributed to the founder of the Confucian tradition, Kongzi (551–479 BCE), who is more commonly referred to as Confucius in the West. Philip J. Ivanhoe argues that the *Analects* is as relevant and important today as it has proven to be over the course of its more than two thousand year history, not only for the people who live in East Asian societies but for all human beings. The fact that this text has inspired so many talented people for so long, across a range of complex, creative, rich, and fascinating cultures offers a strong *prima facie* reason for thinking that the insights the *Analects* contains are not bound by either the particular time or cultural context in which the text took shape.

Philip J. Ivanhoe is Chair Professor of East Asian & Comparative Philosophy & Religion at City University of Hong Kong.

CONFUCIAN REFLECTIONS

Ancient Wisdom for Modern Times

Philip J. Ivanhoe

Routledge
Taylor & Francis Group

NEW YORK AND LONDON

First published 2013
by Routledge
711 Third Avenue, New York, NY 10017

Simultaneously published in the UK
by Routledge
2 Park Square, Milton Park, Abingdon, Oxon OX14 4RN

Routledge is an imprint of the Taylor & Francis Group, an informa business

© 2013 Taylor & Francis

The right of Philip J. Ivanhoe to be identified as author of this
work has been asserted by him/her in accordance with sections
77 and 78 of the Copyright, Designs and Patents Act 1988.

Library of Congress Cataloging-in-Publication Data
  Ivanhoe, P. J.
  Confucian reflections : ancient wisdom for modern times /
  by Philip J. Ivanhoe. — 1 [edition].
    pages cm
  Includes index.
  1. Philosophy, Confucian. 2. Confucius. Lun yu. I. Title.
  B127.C65I93 2014
  181'.112—dc22   2013001347

ISBN: 978-0-415-84487-1 (hbk)
ISBN: 978-0-415-84488-8 (pbk)
ISBN: 978-0-203-74943-2 (ebk)

Typeset in Bembo
by Apex CoVantage, LLC

Printed and bound in the United States of America
by Edwards Brothers Malloy

For Jiang Hong—

My constant companion, greatest inspiration,
and most reliable guide.

CONTENTS

ACKNOWLEDGMENTS

I thank the many teachers, colleagues, students, and friends who have helped me to understand the Confucian tradition and who have shared my enthusiasm for its insights throughout my adult life. I thank the people of Korea, Japan, Taiwan, and China who have shown me the value of Confucian teachings by the harmony, warmth, grace, and wisdom of their daily lives and the generosity, hospitality, and patience they have shown to me over many years and in diverse circumstances and contexts. I thank the ancients in the Confucian tradition and in other world traditions who have taught me so much. Thanks to Daniel A. Bell, Karen L. Carr, Erin M. Cline, Owen J. Flanagan, Fan Ruiping, Sungmoon Kim, Paul Kjellberg, James F. Peterman, Michael R. Slater, Jennifer D. White, and Yu Kam-por, who offered corrections or comments on earlier drafts of this work. Special thanks to Melanie J. Dorson, Justin Tiwald, and Erin M. Cline and Michael R. Slater for carefully reading through and commenting on the entire manuscript; to the Department of Public Policy, City University of Hong Kong for generously supporting this work; and to the *Global Forum on Civilization and Peace* of *The Academy of Korean Studies* for permission to reprint a revised and expanded version of my paper "The Contemporary Significance of Confucian Views about the Ethical Values of Music," which I presented in the Forum's meeting in 2009 and subsequently was published by them in *2009 Civilization and Peace* (Seoul; Edison, NJ: Jimoondang, 2010): 123–33.

CONVENTIONS

For the first occurrence of citations in the footnotes, the full reference is given. For subsequent citations an abbreviated reference to the work is provided.

For the first occurrence of Chinese names and important terms of art I provide the Pinyin Romanization and original Chinese characters in parentheses. For phrases and sentences from Chinese sources, I provide an English translation followed by the Chinese characters in parentheses. For the names of contemporary mainland authors, I use simplified characters. For all traditional names, terms, and texts, I use the traditional forms of the characters.

All translations from Chinese are my own.

PREFACE

This book is about the early Chinese Confucian classic the *Analects* (*Lunyu* 論語), attributed to the founder of the Confucian tradition, a man known as Master Kong (Kongzi 孔子; 551–479 BCE), who is more commonly referred to as Confucius in the West.* Its premise is that Kongzi's *Analects* is as relevant and important today as it has proven to be over the course of its more than two thousand year history, not only for the people who live in East Asian societies but for all human beings.[1] The fact that this text has inspired so many talented people for so long, across a range of complex, creative, rich, and fascinating cultures offers a strong prima facie reason for thinking that the insights the *Analects* contain are not bound by either the particular time or cultural context in which the text took shape.[2] I invite readers to consider the themes explored in the six core chapters of this volume and decide for themselves whether,

---

* A traditional picture of Kongzi appears on the cover of this volume. The horizontal characters at the top say, "An image of Kongzi, the first teacher, spreading his teachings." The two vertical lines on the right say, "His virtue the equal of heaven and earth; His Way crowns both past and present. He edited and disseminated the Six Classics; Handing down a model for all ages."

taken together, they provide a good case for the general importance of Confucianism for contemporary life.

I have spent most of my life writing about the philosophical and religious traditions of East Asia, working to present charitable but historically sensitive translations and accounts of thinkers in the Confucian, Daoist, and Buddhist traditions. I also have done philosophical work that is meant to be applied more directly to modern life, more so-called constructive philosophy, often, though not always, inspired by my study of these traditions. The current volume lies somewhere between the genres of history of philosophy and constructive philosophy. It is not a historical account of Kongzi's philosophy; it is how I see the relevance of some of his teachings for philosophical and social problems in the contemporary world, how I think a modern Confucian might see her or his own tradition.[3] The title *Confucian Reflections* is meant to convey that these are reflections both on and of Kongzi's teachings.

Throughout this work I seek to develop and make plausible and appealing charitable interpretations of core features of Kongzi's teachings. I am consciously and intentionally trying to make *the most* out of the Confucian tradition, because I believe it contains deep and genuine insights. I should not, though, be understood as defending traditionalism or seeking to excuse the very real and at times profound shortcomings and problems with a number of Confucian beliefs and practices. I will note a number of these in the course of my presentation, and it should be clear that I am a critic as well as admirer of this as well as many other traditions. Criticisms of Confucianism and tradition in general shall always remain important, in fact, on the view I endorse and advocate, ongoing criticism and revision is part of every living tradition, but such criticisms are not in short supply or difficult to find. My purpose here is to shed light on some features of the tradition, the constructive and productive potential of which have largely been overlooked or underappreciated.

Philip J. Ivanhoe
City University of Hong Kong
Hong Kong SAR

INTRODUCTION

Early in my career as a teacher of East Asian and comparative philosophy and religion, I assigned one of my very bright and well-educated young graduate students a selection of passages from the *Analects*. His task was to read through these passages in Classical Chinese and come to my office the following week ready to discuss their grammar, meaning, and philosophical importance. My young charge showed up at the appointed time and place and did a fine job explaining the grammar and meaning of the passages he was assigned, but when it came time to discuss their philosophical importance his initial response was less than what I had hoped for. He described the *Analects* as "boring" and "without any relevance to contemporary life." I was disappointed and a bit surprised by these remarks and pointed out to him that the bulk of the text we had before us was at least two thousand years old, parts of it were several hundred years older than that.[1] For thousands of years, the *Analects* has fascinated, sustained, challenged, and inspired many of the brightest and most creative minds in China, Vietnam, Korea, and Japan; in the last few hundred years it has spread to Europe and North America and in more recent times has become a universal global phenomenon.[2] Now, I said to my student, we have to assume that *more than a few* of the people from these diverse cultures and times, who have found this text to be so profound and captivating, were *at least* as smart, creative, caring, and imaginative as we are. If we find it boring and without relevance, our first thought should be: *We must not understand it.*

My student went on to become a successful and widely admired professor of comparative philosophy and a most cherished friend who has taught me and many others much over the years. While by nature and intellectual proclivity more inclined to the *Zhuangzi*, he also came to appreciate the *Analects*, and I am sure—given his character and personality—that this had nothing to do with the fact that I valued it. (If anything, this made it *less* likely or at least more difficult for him to appreciate the text!) He came to value it because in the years that followed we and later he and his colleagues and students read, studied, and discussed the *Analects*, along with other texts from the Chinese and Western traditions, and came to see at least some of the ways in which this ancient classic offers profound and productive insights into the problems we, our friends, family members, and fellow human beings, still confront in the very different places and times in which we live.

There are of course parts of the *Analects* that do not have any direct bearing on how we do or should live our lives today— except, perhaps, by showing us what *not* to do and how *not* to be. For example, I don't think many informed and reasonable people who have a choice in the matter would choose to live under an absolute king rather than under some form of representative government, with all its shortcomings, nor do I think that any informed, caring, and reasonable person should tolerate, much less endorse, the general view of women that one finds, at least by implication, in the *Analects*.[3] Even in the case of these negative lessons, there often is something of great importance to learn and ponder, but such issues will not serve as the focus of the present study. Instead, I shall concentrate on six prominent themes in the *Analects* that are of singular value for contemporary people. I mean by this that these are issues we tend to ignore, to the detriment of ourselves as well as others, and into which we can gain significant insight by studying and implementing ideas described in the *Analects*.

Studying, practicing, and mastering any worthwhile body of knowledge can give rise to a distinctive and often neglected sense of comfort, satisfaction, and joy. This feeling comes from many sources; ultimately it is grounded in the ancient and indispensable need to survive, find a way through, and, as best we can, master the challenges of our natural environment. It is found in and comes to us in different forms: from the experience we all have had of coming to understand and implement any challenging and powerful new idea or skill, to the more rare but equally intelligible sense of grasping and putting into practice some deep insight about human life, what is properly called wisdom. This sense of satisfaction and joy is an important part of what Kongzi calls the "love of learning" (好學). The *Analects* begins with the line, "Is it not a joy to study and at the proper time practice what one has learned?" (學而時習之不亦悅乎) (*Analects* 1.1). I take this as the epigraph, motto, and inspiration for this volume.

In the opening section of Book Seven of the *Analects*, Kongzi describes himself as "One who transmits rather than creates; one who trusts in and loves the ancients" (述而不作信而好古). From its very inception, Kongzi's "Way" (*dao* 道) was explicitly committed to defending a particular form of life: a culture, or more specifically a *tradition*.[4] It is important, though, to keep in mind that the tradition he sought to defend and promote was not the dominant culture of his time; he sought to preserve and revitalize a tradition that was largely lost and discredited. He was committed to a mission of revival and reinvigoration, not conserving the status quo. Down to the present day, Confucians have insisted on defending this historical lineage; they make no attempt to disguise the fact that they are participants in and advocates of an ongoing tradition of thought, belief, and practice.[5] The traditional aspects of Confucianism are undeniable, and this has been the source of many modern criticisms. In chapter one of this book, "Being in and Learning from Tradition," I begin our study of the *Analects* by offering a partial defense of Kongzi's advocacy of tradition, arguing that a modern Confucian perspective on traditions shows how essential they are to human flourishing. While there is no denying the fact that traditions can constrain human creativity and stifle individual expression, I show that these negative aspects of certain historical traditions are not in any way inherent to the notion of what a tradition is or can be.

It is simply wrong to claim, as many do, that past misuses of tradition offer a reasonable warrant to reject tradition altogether. We see arguments of this kind leveled against patriotism or religion as well, and the arguments are equally bad. Just because some people in the past have used tradition, love of country, and religious belief for bad ends is no reason to equate any of these with the bad ends themselves, or to ignore all the other goods these embody and can bring to human lives. Such an argument could be used to criticize just about *anything*. People have used scissors and rope to commit murder but neither scissors nor rope is murder nor do they inexorably lead to or encourage murder. They should not be blamed and banned because *some* people have misused them. Moreover, these past misapplications should not lead us to overlook all the good and wonderful things scissors and rope have and continue to do for us. Such misguided criticisms of tradition have given rise to a more general condemnation and rejection of tradition, at least within many modern liberal societies. This is unfortunate, because it tends to lead us to ignore, disparage, and throw overboard unique and important aspects of our humanity. One might be able to support a blanket rejection of tradition if one could show that there is something *inherent* in the concept or practice of tradition itself that inevitably leads to a preponderance of bad consequences. To the best of my knowledge, though, no one has attempted, much less successfully made such an argument. Confucianism offers us valuable resources for rethinking the nature of tradition and the many positive roles it can play in our lives; this is the theme and focus of our opening chapter.

Chapter two, "Conceptions of Self, Society, and World," explores the connections between our self-conception and the complex relationships we have with other people, creatures, and the world at large. Western thinkers like Kierkegaard, Heidegger, and Sartre have convincingly argued that a self is not a static entity; it doesn't have a fixed nature that determines all it is and does.[6] Human beings are not like tables and chairs—things that simply exist *in themselves* but rather are creatures that live *for themselves*—and this difference is immensely significant. Unlike tables and chairs, human beings play an important part in determining *for themselves* what they do and what they become. Nevertheless, Confucians insist that we do not determine what we are for ourselves *by ourselves*, a meaningful life is not just something I can declare or decide on my own.[7] Just as the meaning of words does not exist in my head, the meaning of life is not something I alone determine: it depends upon wider social ideals, norms, and practices and these reflect critical and fundamental aspects of human nature.[8] Confucians would further insist that I do not just decide *for myself* how to live. As a member of a larger society, my choices influence others, both directly and indirectly. The choices we make about fundamental features of a good or decent life express not only what we want for *ourselves* but what we think any person should want or at least should have access to. One implication of this way of thinking leads to a characteristic feature of Confucianism: the idea that the best kind of life we can have is an explicitly social life, a life that is lived fulfilling complex relationships with other people, creatures, and things.

A common modern view of happiness inclines us to seek for happiness by focusing on the pursuit of a narrow set of personal interests. The basic idea is that the more desires and preferences I can fulfill, the happier I shall be. Confucianism rejects such a view and insists first that we must reflect upon the desires we happen to have: in their view, the mere possession of a desire is not, in itself, good reason to fulfill it much less a good reason to think that fulfilling it will lead you to be happy. If we begin this process of reflection, Confucians believe we will be led to see that many desires are not really *desirable* at all. Once we see their consequences, for ourselves and others, a number of our desires will cause us to feel ashamed of harboring them and to realize that we need to turn away from them and dedicate ourselves to becoming the kind of person who does not *have*, much less seeks to fulfill, such desires.[9] Nevertheless, this does not lead Confucians to advocate the elimination of all desires; to the contrary, they see the ideal life as firmly tied to the development and fulfillment of the right kinds of desires. Confucians maintain that if we study the people around us and read accounts of other possible ways to live, as well as continually reflect upon the full range of desires we happen to have, we will find that cultivating certain desires and taking on ideals we don't presently have can lead us to much more satisfying and fulfilling lives. If we commit ourselves to the protracted and challenging process of cultivating ourselves, we can improve ourselves and find new satisfactions and rewards in life. The basic idea is similar to the common view that developing certain skills, tastes, and preferences enriches human life. Those who can play an instrument well, appreciate different forms and traditions of art, and prefer poetry to pick-up sticks are, other things being equal, leading richer and better lives and contributing more to the lives of those around them.

Confucians believe the form of life they advocate holds the promise of certain highly desirable advantages. On the one hand, a life in harmony with the Way offers a sense of being free from a range of common human concerns, fears, and anxieties; on the other hand, it produces a sense of being part of something more grand and significant than any individual project or pleasure could possibly afford. A commitment to the Way requires one to see oneself and one's happiness as organically related to and in common cause with the lives of other people, creatures, and things.[10] Advancing along the Way leads one to cast off and leave behind the narrowly focused, self-interested views of self and happiness that define many modern, consumer-oriented lives. One loses or sloughs off this earlier self as one develops and embraces a more expansive sense of oneself. From this latter perspective, one's earlier conceptions of self and happiness no longer hold any appeal and appear as what they are: immature, wanting, overly self-centered, and unworthy of attention. This new, more expansive sense of self roughly describes the Confucian conception of what it is to be a good person and how such people see their relationships to the people, creatures, and things of the world in which they live.

Chapter three, "Social Practices Great and Small," is devoted to a better understanding and deeper appreciation of Confucian "ritual" (*li* 禮) and its relevance for contemporary life. There is some similarity between modern attitudes toward ritual and tradition: both tend to be disparaged as largely empty, pointless, and inimical to individual welfare and happiness. In this chapter, I mount a concerted defense of ritual not only as something that in fact permeates and informs our modern life but also as something we need to appreciate and about which we need to reflect: both to preserve, nurture, and enhance the rituals we already have and to create and pursue new ones. Like our notion of self or the nature of our traditions, rituals are not fixed and unchanging aspects of human life; while addressing fundamental human needs and engaging basic capacities, they are very much artifacts of our collective ingenuity; we need to continually revise and invent as well as follow and appreciate our rituals as well as our traditions.

Confucians have focused a great deal of sustained attention upon ritual and have deep and important insights about this aspect of human life. One could make a good case for claiming that the Confucian tradition itself lies more in its rituals and classical texts than in any set of beliefs or propositions, but this is something equally true of *most* religious traditions.[11] This claim should not be taken as in any way entailing or implying that such traditions are static, stale, or inflexible. Anyone who has even a cursory understanding of Confucianism, or any other venerable tradition, knows that its practices and texts have evolved over time and continue to be reinterpreted in the course of their unfolding. A number of modern Western scholars have recognized both the central place ritual has played in Confucian cultures as well as the importance of ritual in our modern lives, and this recognition plays a central role in the contemporary revival of Confucianism that is occurring throughout East Asia today.[12] This chapter is informed by and seeks to contribute to this revived interest in ritual.

Chapter four, "Music in and of Our Lives," draws upon the Confucian tradition to initiate an exploration of some of the ways music has and continues to play a role in our lives. Modern people tend to think of music exclusively as a form of entertainment and personal expression, but Confucians have understood music as having more serious and greater social dimensions as well; in light of such beliefs, they have developed powerful and revealing views about the nature and function of music. In this chapter, I not only describe and analyze some of these traditional Confucian beliefs but also argue that versions of them should inform and guide our own understanding of the ways that music can shape and express our feelings, beliefs, and actions. Music is entertaining, but often it is much more than this, and its subtle, swift, and profound influence upon us is well worth greater attention and careful reflection.

Confucians have argued that among its many uses, music can serve as a diagnostic: a way to gauge and gain a sense for important ideals or themes in individual lives and within the broader societies in which people live. According to this view, if one were to sample the music a person listens to or creates or the music that is most popular in a given society or age, it would provide important insights into what kinds of ideals and issues animate the lives of these people. The themes of the music as well as many features of the music itself can reveal what occupies and animates the lives of the people. To put it a bit roughly, when times are hard, people are more likely to sing the blues; if they are struggling for equality or justice, themes of protest, resistance, and liberation tend to inform and inspire their music; if they are committed to war, their music will reflect a martial spirit;[13] if they are at peace, it will celebrate the joys and aspirations of daily human life. In addition to this diagnostic function, music can serve a didactic purpose as well: it often expresses, influences, and shapes the ideals and aspirations that people live by. Contrary to the dominant contemporary view of music as simply a form of entertainment, traditional Chinese thinkers recognized that music has subtle, swift, and often profound power to influence how we think, feel, and act. This is something that has been used and abused by political and social movements throughout human history but it is a lesson largely ignored and often forgotten in our everyday lives. The music we listen to and create works upon us and those around us; it can orient, excite, and inspire us in various ways, for good and bad. Confucians insist that the music in and of our lives is much more important than most moderns tend to believe and urge us to reflect upon and choose wisely the rhythms and melodies that inform and enliven our lives.

Chapter Five, "The Values of Families," is dedicated to what is widely regarded as the most characteristic feature of the Confucian tradition: its focus upon and dedication to families.[14] While it is true that Confucians have always been greatly concerned with and placed tremendous value upon families, it is simply wrong to think that these issues are neglected in other cultures and traditions or that they are no longer of great and fundamental importance even in the liberal societies within which some ignore, criticize, or dismiss their significance.[15] My concern in this chapter is to explore some of the distinctive reasons Confucians give for according such pride of place to families and to argue that versions of at least a number of these traditional beliefs remain convincing and even compelling today.

One of the most important roles families play in human life is in the acquisition of our basic moral sensibilities. The earliest periods of life offer us the first opportunities we have to develop a sense of ourselves as related to others, our first experiences of being loved for who we are, and our first dim understandings of our mutual interdependence and the related desire to live in harmony with other human beings and by extension the rest of the world.[16] Given the importance such early childhood experiences play in the formation of our basic ethical sensibilities, it is quite reasonable to see families, broadly construed, as one of the most critical features of our ethical landscape, but families make other unique and important contributions to our ethical lives as well. They are where we often are at our most vulnerable and in need of help and where we most regularly are called upon to and bestow care. These features of families have important implications for a range of ethical, social, and political issues. For example, they offer clear and persuasive reasons for affording families special status within society: an issue at the heart of the so-called public-private debate in contemporary ethical and political theory. The modern Confucian perspective that I describe and defend in this chapter insists that it is wrong to draw a clear, bright, and impermeable line between families and the rest of society, as many modern Western thinkers tend to do. From the Confucian point of view, families serve as the "inner" domestic core around which the "outer" public world is wrapped; these two spheres of life are parts of a single, organically related continuum across which we regularly cross and within which we work out and live our lives.[17] The world is not sharply divided into contrasting realms of a loving, nurturing, and all-forgiving domestic realm and a fierce, competitive, and punishing social world. Most elements of each of these spheres of life can be found in the other, in one form or another. A distinctive and important feature of the Confucian view of these different parts of life is that the virtues we need in one sphere, in large measure, are the same as those we need in the other. Such a belief motivates the Confucian ideal of developing virtue within the family and gradually extending it out to embrace and encompass larger and larger parts of the world beyond; it is also the idea underlying characteristically Confucian descriptions of the state as, roughly, the family writ large.

In our sixth and final chapter, "Awareness, Attentiveness, and Care in and of the Everyday," I seek to draw attention to some less explicit but fundamentally important features of the Confucian tradition. The central claim of this chapter is that while Confucians aim at grand goals, they take their stand, work out of, and remain grounded in the everyday. Their ultimate aim is remarkably ambitious and at times even quite utopian: seeking to transform the world for the better. Nevertheless, they insist that we pursue this lofty goal by beginning with the most accessible and familiar features of human life: working to develop the self by concentrating on what we see, do, think, and say in the course of each and every day.

Their approach is not just an instrumental strategy, an efficient way to achieve more lofty goals. Working on the everyday makes a critical contribution to the greater good and partly constitutes it; it is not just a ladder or stairway leading to some higher plane, state, or place that one leaves behind after ascending. Moreover, as one works to make one's everyday life better, one comes to see the necessity of working to make better the larger social context within which one's life is led. Focusing on the everyday leads Confucians to develop a range of fascinating views about what we might generally describe as meditation, in the sense of a dynamic, critical, and reflective practice rather than a formal posture-based regimen of training. Much of the work of Confucian self-cultivation requires us to become highly aware, watchful, disciplined, and attuned, we must learn to pay attention to and carefully guide and craft our thoughts, feelings, postures, expressions, and actions to be in accord with the Way. The opening chapter of the *Doctrine of the Mean* (*Zhongyong* 中庸) teaches, "Cultivated individuals carefully watch over themselves" (君子慎其獨). This effort, though, is not purely introspective; the core of the project of cultivating the self lies in the challenge of developing much greater levels of awareness, attentiveness, and care in regard to the quotidian aspects of life as well as to one's inner thoughts and feelings.

The themes described immediately above are implied in the issues we have explored in the previous five chapters: we are to work on improving the traditions that inform our lives, understand and work to relate the self to society and the world, focus on social practices great and small, be aware of, attend to, and take care about the music we create and listen to, endeavor to fulfill our obligations to those closest and most dear to us and work to extend such care out to all under heaven. In this final chapter, I seek to show the importance of the everyday not only to the practical work of Confucian cultivation but also to its conception of the nature of and way to its ultimate goals. Confucians insist that one cannot work toward the grand goal of improving the world by rejecting or neglecting the everyday: the former may be their greatest aspiration but it will be realized only by ensuring that it is pursued within an environment conducive to growth and working to tend and nurture the roots that give rise to and support this result. The Way is grounded and realized in the daily challenges and joys of normal human life.

The Confucian tradition has informed and inspired major East Asian cultures for more than two thousand years and now has spread beyond this vast, diverse, and complex region and is known throughout the world. Despite its innate value, remarkable longevity, and continued vitality, it is largely ignored by Western-ers, aside from a small number of academics, most of whom study Confucianism as a purely historical phenomenon. While these scholars have consistently produced work of exceptional quality, sophistication, and value, this exclusive disciplinary orientation re-inforces the widely shared impression of Confucianism as a rem-nant of the past, an ossified specimen of an exotic culture that has faded from memory and now lives in the academic equivalent of museums, covered with dust. The truth is Confucianism has never faded from the hearts and minds of East Asian people; it is currently experiencing a remarkable revival, manifested in many different facets of East Asian culture, especially in contemporary China. From every indication, it is not only here to stay but sure to continue flourishing. This volume seeks to explain some of the reasons why it has proven to possess such profound and enduring attractiveness and generated such dedicated commitment among East Asian people and argues that these features of Confucian-ism are relevant and important not only to them but to all of us. Confucianism is a personal ethic and spiritual path as well as a social and political philosophy and true to its generally organic approach to such issues, it insists that these pursuits are inseparable. For Confucianism as well as for many contemporary feminists, "the personal is the political." In addition, for Confucians, as well as for many religious practitioners, "the secular is sacred." My study of the Confucian tradition, like my study of just about everything I have written on, has also often been personal as well as profes-sional, sacred as well as secular. I have not only sought to under-stand, describe, and analyze Confucian philosophy but have always reflected on what it might mean not only to those who follow this Way but to me and others both dear and unfamiliar to me who are not Confucians. This work reflects not only what I have learned but also some of the ways in which I have changed in the course of my study, for I have come to believe in, adopt, and implement in my life many of the lessons I shall endeavor to describe in the following chapters.

1

BEING IN AND LEARNING FROM TRADITION

For thousands of years, scholars from different cultures and times have offered a wide range of competing views, conflicting interpretations, opinions, and judgments about Confucianism, but they agree on at least one thing: it is a complex and venerable *tradition*, a collection of beliefs, texts, norms, habits, and practices handed down from one generation to the next. Kongzi made no attempt to disguise this feature of his Way; as noted in the Introduction, he once described himself as "one who transmits rather than creates; one who trusts in and loves the ancients" (*Analects* 7.1). Today, however, fidelity to tradition is not widely regarded as a virtue. Many people in modern, industrialized societies harbor and express the view that tradition, in whatever form it might take, is a remnant of past ages, a world well lost, a drag or constraint on freedom and creativity and an obstacle to living a satisfying and happy life. Some who believe this to be true may provide reasons for holding such beliefs, but we might and should ask if they have *good* reasons to do so.[1]

No one can deny that there are cases in which traditions cramp, hamstring, or even smother our attempts to live well. Not every tradition is worthy of support or worth defending; traditions can regress or devolve as well as improve over time; they can ossify into traditionalism, which, as we shall discuss below, is both unappealing and unworthy of support. Even when traditions go wrong, though, this can and in most cases should be viewed as a challenge to correct, strengthen, and enhance the given tradition rather than a reason to abandon it altogether. As noted in the Introduction, even though traditions have proven to have flaws and have been misused to support bad ends, this does not come close to offering good reasons to ignore or abandon them. This is especially clear when we come to appreciate the fact that, as human beings, we cannot avoid living in and through traditions; we begin, pass through, and end our lives connected to traditions of various kinds.[2] Rather than a constraint upon freedom and creativity, traditions offer the only chance we have for creative and original lives; in addition, they can be unique sources for deep and important senses of identity, connection, and satisfaction.

There is a significant difference between living through a tradition and embracing traditionalism. The former arguably is an unavoidable feature of human life; the latter is a retreat from a fully human life. We live through our traditions when we carry them forward in a reverent but critical attitude, reforming, improving, and refining them as the need arises. We suffer under traditionalism when because of coercion, fear, or a lack of imagination we mindlessly accept and perpetuate the beliefs and practices of the past. Jaroslav Pelikan captured these ideas perfectly and beautifully when he wrote that "tradition is the living faith of the dead, traditionalism is the dead faith of the living. And, I suppose I should add, it is traditionalism that gives tradition such a bad name."[3]

I will argue that traditions are much more pervasive in our lives than we realize and in doing so foreshadow a similar argument I will make in regard to rituals. In making this case, I rely upon a distinction between implicit, or latent, traditions and explicit, or manifest, traditions. Just as there is a difference between regular and important shared practices that we at least sometimes call "rituals" and the formal rituals of established religions, there are more loosely organized, historically extended movements or practices that can and at times are thought of as traditions that differ from explicit traditions such as Roman Catholicism or Confucianism. For example, we don't think it unusual to talk about traditions of scientific inquiry, peaceful protest, or musical performance even though these usually lack the social recognition and institutionalized forms of celebration that we find in established religious traditions. This suggests there is a set of related phenomena forming a spectrum between more latent and more explicit traditions. I believe that this is correct and moreover will argue that we should not only recognize this fact about our lives but in some cases we should work to transform more latent traditions into more explicit ones.

We cannot live good human lives without participating in traditions any more than we can live good human lives without learning and using a language.[4] A human language itself is an example of a latent tradition and a critical feature of every culture. Like other traditions, human languages are products of long processes of accretion and accumulation, not the result of any single episode of creation or the reflection of a particular theory about what a language should be. We all are shaped by the linguistic and larger cultural traditions in which we are raised and to some extent we are constrained by them. They are, however, the very media through which we understand ourselves, each other, and the world around us; they also are the source of tremendous security, satisfaction, meaning, and joy. They are not prisons—unless *we* make or allow them to be so; they offer us a place to stand, a vantage point upon the world where we begin our reflections and dialogues with others about the shape, significance, and tempo of human lives. The question is not whether to live within traditions; the question is *how* best to do so.

Traditions of various kinds are not parts of the natural world; they are human constructs, but they are nonetheless real; the same can be said of human language or culture in general, and these offer many of the most meaningful, pleasing, and satisfying experiences human beings can have.[5] Why is it then that so many modern people acquire at least a mild and often strong antagonism toward tradition while often being only dimly aware of the sources of such animosity and the degree to which such an attitude can needlessly complicate and often diminish the quality of their lives? Perhaps the first thing to say on this topic has been noted above in Pelikan's revealing distinction between tradition and traditionalism; the latter is the source of much contemporary animosity. The second thing might be that a negative attitude toward tradition is largely a contingent and distinctive feature of our place in history. Rather than representing a long and widely held view expressing some deep insight into the human condition or the key to happiness, the failure to appreciate tradition is a highly anomalous and an almost certainly temporary feature of modern liberal societies—one that might well be on the wane even within these cultures but even today is by no means a uniform or universal view. Vital and vibrant traditions are the norm in most of the world's civilizations even in contemporary times, and traditions of various kinds are central to some extent in many people's lives, even within the most liberal modern societies. Future generations surely will be perplexed by some of our most passionately held beliefs and practices, such as the widespread acceptance among contemporary intellectuals of "economic man," *Homo Economicus*—the idea that by nature human beings most regularly seek to maximize their individual material welfare[6]—and the related general antagonism people in our time tend to show toward tradition. I venture to suggest—and hope—that both these features of modernity will come to be seen as expression of the *zeitgeist* of an anomalous, overly self-centered and inadequately reflective period in human history.

The case of the Confucian tradition is not wholly unlike the case of Christianity in that both traditions came under considerable criticism, some of it clearly justified, with the rise of the modern world.[7] The twentieth century marked an age of magnificent advancement in many important areas of human life. In particular the wicked and appalling nature of discrimination based on race, sex, and class was revealed, challenged, and to varying degrees overturned, at least across a range of modern cultures.[8] These achievements did not come without great struggle and sacrifice and constitute a legacy we all should appreciate, guard, celebrate, and carry forward. Many of these movements are latent traditions and offer some of the best candidates for elevation to explicit traditions. Recognizing that these great social movements have founding figures, defining moments, characteristic themes, and a discernible historical trajectory is the first step toward embracing them as explicit traditions.

Two important facts must not escape our attention. First, as long as we continue to learn more about ourselves and our world, it is *inevitable* that parts of our current as well as past beliefs, practices, and norms—including those that are parts of our traditions—shall come to be seen as ill-founded. Second, as long as we remain on earth and continue to live as intelligent, inquisitive, and creative creatures, we will be able to improve the traditions that define our various modes of life. On the other hand, we will always face the possibility of falling into future dark ages if we fail to live up to the best features and employ the most noble capacities of our species, if we forsake our traditions and retreat into traditionalism or disperse into chaos.

Our progress and advancements do not simply emerge out of the void—progress without history is a modern conceit and delusion; they are developments and improvements that, in almost every case, arise from and in one way or another continue ongoing traditions, both latent and explicit. Even in instances where there is a sudden and dramatic break with the past, the form a protest or revolution takes is largely defined in terms of what it responds to and in this respect the former tradition informs and shapes the new beliefs, norms, and practices that emerge and often lives on in various other ways in people's memories, attitudes, and behaviors. In these various ways, the past always shapes our present and influences the trajectory of the future. Many modern people have a tendency to suffer from an illusion we might call *temporal provincialism*, the belief that our present understanding of the world is somehow definitive and exceedingly superior to anything that has or will ever be known. History provides us ample illustrations of the folly of such a conceit; consider what happened to Europe after the collapse of the Roman Empire. The great Confucian philosopher Zhang Xuecheng (章學誠) (1738–1801), warned against such temporal provincialism saying,[9] "a hundred years from now, we too will be 'someone from the past.' Put yourself in the place of posterity and consider how we will fare?" (百年之後吾輩亦古人也設身處地又當如何).

The case of women's liberation in the West, which has grown into a global though by no means universal phenomenon, offers a splendid example of a latent tradition that should be embraced as an explicit tradition. The great movement that identified, challenged, and overturned the massively unjust, deeply misguided, and thoroughly odious constellation of attitudes, beliefs, practices and norms that oppressed and exploited women, harmed them profoundly, and indirectly made everyone's lives much less noble and fulfilling was and remains a prolonged struggle; while revolutionary in its implications and effects, it was not a revolution in terms of its process, if we conceive of revolution as an abrupt overthrow and break with the past. It was inspired and sustained by beliefs that already were widely held within a range of societies, beliefs about the fundamental freedom, dignity, and equality of all human beings. What it sought and insisted upon was that these deep truths be extended fully to women. The same is true of the magnificent struggles collectively known as the *civil rights movement*; is this not another prime candidate for elevation to the status of explicit tradition? These profound social transformations were and continue to be movements forged in trenchant insight, careful planning, and sustained courageous action. They succeeded only through great effort, time, and sacrifice, and like most good things are not wholly complete, perfect, or secure.

The women's liberation movement is constituted by the commitment of many people, some well-known, many mostly unknown, a series of events, some great and some small, and a set of institutions, both local and global, which together form a *tradition*: an organized, reflective, and intentional collection of ideas and activities that is handed down and extends through time. Seeing that the movement is at least a latent tradition is important for a number of distinctive reasons, which lie at the heart of the concerns of this chapter. First, such a conception explains the remarkable devotion, pride, and satisfaction that so many people feel, to varying degrees, toward the achievements and aims of women's liberation. Second seeing this movement as a tradition can help us to keep in our hearts and minds those with great insight and imagination who worked and sacrificed to make our lives and societies better. We must not forget the founding figures of this tradition—women like Mary Wollstonecraft and Elizabeth Cady Stanton (the latter, a major figure in the abolitionist movement as well)—all that they sacrificed and all that they achieved. Their images do and should appear in our books, but they should also be displayed on our currency and in our parks and public places, and their memories should remain forever etched upon our hearts. We should publicly recognize and collectively celebrate them and their work in regular shared ceremonies. We should embrace them and their work as an important tradition. This is only fitting; it is also terribly important as a source of inspiration for contemporary and future members of this and every proud tradition. Kongzi always sought to *keep in mind* the sages and other exemplary figures of his tradition and all that they achieved. He was disconcerted whenever he felt he was losing a vivid sense and connection to the great figures of the past; one day he exclaimed, "Too long has it been, since I dreamed of seeing the Duke of Zhou!" (久矣吾不復夢見周公) (*Analects* 7.5).[10]

Understanding women's liberation *as a tradition* helps us focus our attention on the need to remain vigilant, to guard the progress that has been made and seek to carry it forward: we should revere and feel the need to prove worthy of our inheritance. When we study the tradition we will be impressed not only with the insight and courage of those who forged it, but also by the arc of its trajectory, which continues into the present day and will pass beyond it. The early insights of this tradition are clearly the achievements of "someone from the past," and, as Zhang Xuecheng so trenchantly observed, it is easy to criticize the views and actions of earlier figures from the privileged perspective of later history. We should remember, though, that this later, more enlightened perspective is not the final word and is something *they* bequeathed unto us. A fair assessment of their achievements in light of this historical fact will impress any reflective and reasonable person and can motivate us both to carry the struggle forward and recognize our own and others' limitations. We should learn from and improve upon Goethe's advice, "Take what you have inherited from your fathers and work to make it your own" (*Was du ererbt von deinen Vaetern hast, Erwirb es um es zu besitzen*).[11] We should take what we have inherited from our *mothers* (and fathers) and work to make it our own. This is precisely what it is to live through tradition.

The tradition of women's liberation should also inspire us to be attentive and aware, to seek out cases where we fail to treat others with the justice, dignity, and care that we owe to all human beings. Cultivating and maintaining an awareness of and attentiveness to the world around one as well as to one's inner thoughts and feelings, in the course of one's everyday activities and in light of traditional ideals and exemplars, is an important part of the Confucian tradition. As noted in the Introduction, the opening chapter of the *Doctrine of the Mean* teaches that "cultivated individuals carefully watch over themselves." We shall return to explore further the need to develop and maintain this kind of awareness, attentiveness, and care in the sixth and final chapter of this work.

Seeing the women's liberation movement not only as a tradition within modern societies but as one of its most valuable and distinctive characteristics is absolutely essential for the ultimate, sustained success of its noble and edifying aims. Only when we *all* explicitly see this tradition as part of *our* shared commitment, as part of our history, something every one of us is proud of, dedicated to defending, and delighted to celebrate will the vision and dream of the movement's founding figures be realized. Traditions are not simply things to be viewed in museums, from the outside, or claimed or clung to for prestige and safety; they are forms of life that need to be lived out and extended through active and creative participation. As Kongzi teaches us, "Human beings can broaden and extend the Way. The Way cannot broaden and extend human beings" (人能弘道非道能弘人) (*Analects* 15.29; Cf. 19.2).

If one has had the good fortune of receiving a proper education—as one can in many parts of the world today—by the time one completes secondary school, one already has a good grounding in geometry, algebra, and calculus. We often don't consider just how remarkable this is or what has made such achievement possible, but a moment's reflection will reveal that such students, even those without remarkable mathematical talent, know more mathematics than all but the most gifted mathematicians in human history. Great mathematicians like Euclid did not understand algebra or calculus; those were much later achievements and depended on ideas that came from outside the Western tradition of mathematics—ideas like the concept of zero. The reason a good high school student today knows such a vast range of mathematical knowledge is because she inherits a tradition of mathematical inquiry that for many centuries has been a global legacy: the combined insights of a series of remarkably gifted human beings from a variety of cultures and times. She is the inheritor of and a participant in a latent yet ongoing *intellectual tradition* of mathematical inquiry: a magnificent, living human legacy. Whether we consider this a latent or explicit tradition depends greatly upon our involvement with and enthusiasm for mathematics. Those deeply involved in the discipline might consider elevating their love and practice of mathematics into an explicit tradition both to more deeply understand and enjoy what they already are devoted to but also to help manifest and explain the object of their devotion to those less knowledgeable or dedicated.

Another reason our young mathematician knows so much is because she has been *taught* well; she owes her remarkable level of understanding to teachers who passed on the tradition of mathematics. Such teachers play a too often neglected and vastly undervalued role in the perpetuation of human knowledge; it is they who come closest to or fully appreciate mathematics or other disciplines of knowledge as traditions.[12] Through their skill in teaching, their care for their students, and their devotion to and delight in mathematics, they impart not only knowledge but also what Kongzi, the "first teacher," called a *love of learning*. Such devotion to study was highly prized by Kongzi; it was the personal virtue of which he was most proud. He once said, "Even in a hamlet of only ten families you can find someone as conscientious and trustworthy as me, but you won't find anyone who loves learning as much as I do" (十室之邑必有忠信如丘者焉不如丘之好學也) (*Analects* 5.28).[13] Our good high school student possesses a vast treasury of mathematical knowledge because she inherited a tradition of mathematical inquiry that is preserved and propagated by a guild of dedicated teachers. The great geniuses of the coming generation shall emerge from among the ranks of their students.

The very high regard that Confucians have for teachers is an integral and essential feature of their larger view of traditions, for no tradition can survive and flourish without the leadership and inspiration they provide. Good teachers play a critical role at every level of one's education, and we fail them and ourselves when we do not honor and revere the contributions they make and recognize them for what they are and achieve. Every modern Confucian society celebrates the role of teachers on Teacher's Day, a state recognized holiday, and every culture on earth should adopt and institute a similar practice. Such recognition not only is fitting for all that good teachers do; it gives every one of us an opportunity to pause and appreciate their contributions and the multitude of effects these have upon all our lives; it also inspires teachers to live up to the high and noble ideal that is their calling at its best. Such regular, shared public celebration is an important, constitutive element of all traditions.

The example of mathematical understanding illustrates a number of important aspects of the Confucian view of tradition. It shows the degree to which we live in and through traditions; we swim in traditions as fish do in the sea, which helps explain why we often fail to notice them. This tendency to lose sight of the importance of tradition is unfortunate and why the Confucian emphasis upon tradition and the role of teachers is inherently important, particularly timely, and eminently wise. If we fail to think about how much of what we know about critical fields of knowledge such as mathematics is an inheritance, reverently and often joyfully passed down to us, we can develop the delusion that we somehow did or at least could have come to this knowledge on our own. While not conceptually impossible, as a practical matter, it is wildly improbable to believe that any one person could develop, on her own, even the level of mathematics that our good high school student has. If we don't appreciate this fact adequately, we risk losing sight of how important it is to preserve, support, and develop our traditions and teachers; we fail to notice how complex and important are our many relationships with people, both living and dead. We might fail to see the absolutely essential role played by institutions that support learning—from day care and public libraries, publishers and bookstores, to schools, colleges, and universities. Such a view leaves us cut off from the legacy of history and alienated from the extended community of practitioners that constitute the contemporary expression of the tradition of mathematics and other traditions of human learning as well. We can lose a sense of ourselves as parts of these larger, grander human institutions and the traditions they support and mistakenly come to believe we are the sole authors and only source of all that we achieve. This degree of ignorance and misperception manifests more than even a profound lack of knowledge; it represents a complex intellectual and moral vice.

The example of mathematics shows that traditions and teachers play an essential and often underappreciated part in our lives. Next, I would like to focus on the ways in which traditions like mathematics offer us the only chance we have for creative and original lives. The case is really quite evident and compelling. For contrary to the popular view of traditions as absolutely ossified and exclusively constricting prisons of the spirit, it is obvious that learning a tradition like mathematics is a necessary part of many of our most cherished and respected, most original, powerful, and creative intellectual disciplines. Mathematics plays an essential role in every natural and special science; it is the basic language of many of our most profound and productive approaches to knowledge. One need not be a highly creative mathematician in order to appreciate and apply mathematics in creative and revealing ways. Many highly skilled mathematicians and most of the best teachers of mathematics do not advance the field of mathematics in any fundamental way, but they do carry on the tradition of mathematics by relying upon it in the course of their work, making use of it through novel and productive applications, and passing it on to others in creative and inspiring ways.

The same account of the nature and role of tradition applies to endeavors such as painting or music as well. Contrary to images that one often finds in the popular imagination, great artists and musicians don't fall from the sky, spring full-blown from the head of Zeus, or bring themselves into being; they are born of mothers; they learn and are encouraged by parents, teachers, friends, and colleagues, and find inspiration and direction from traditions of painting and music. The origin of their art—its guiding practices, norms, and even the instruments needed to engage in it—are things they inherit. Every student of art starts off studying, copying, and at some level being inspired by past masters, usually under the watchful eye of a teacher. Every musician begins with scales, learns to play increasingly sophisticated compositions, and emulates or borrows from the style of the best musicians she or he can find. In both painting and music, artists discover original and creative ways of expressing themselves through these traditional forms. In some cases, they develop their skills in ways that lead them to move beyond tradition and at times in ways that challenge and alter tradition.[14] But even in such cases, two things cannot be denied. First, that the great artist could never have achieved what she did without passing through the tradition. Second, every successful case in which a great genius goes beyond a tradition is not transcendence in the strong sense of existing or arising from some separate realm or ex nihilo but rather a *new stage* in an actual and ongoing tradition. We live in and through traditions; we need not nor should we be bound or constricted by them.

The early Confucian Xunzi offers a highly original and insightful analysis of the roles tradition can play in human life.[15] One of the most remarkable claims he makes is that an appreciation of our connection with and debt to tradition can *deepen* our sense of satisfaction in life. Xunzi argues that only those who recognize that most of the activities in which they engage and which they enjoy are parts of an ongoing tradition find full satisfaction in what they do. Only such people see themselves and what they do as part of a long and majestic lineage. And so, for example, while it is not in any way necessary for a contemporary musician to know and appreciate the tradition of which she is a part, Xunzi insists not only that she in fact *is* a member of such a tradition, but also that she will know and appreciate both her art and herself more fully when she comes to realize and embrace this fact.[16]

The modern tendency to desire and value breaking free from tradition and standing apart from history represents an exaggerated response to traditions that did indeed inflict oppressive and ossified visions of human life upon people. Traditionalism in the sense of a narrow and dogmatic ideology is something we all can do without. Kongzi explicitly rejects such a point of view: "Cultivated individuals do not approve or oppose any particular cause under heaven; they join in what is right" (君子之於天下也無適 也無莫也義之與比) (*Analects* 4.10; Cf. *Analects* 9.4). The clearest marks of traditionalism is its characteristic defensiveness and self-righteousness, the ways in which it functions almost exclusively to preserve and protect itself and control others rather than working to edify human beings and enhance the lives they lead. Those who embrace traditionalism are easily recognized by the extent to which they are in the grip of a set of beliefs and practices and must employ deception or coercion to hold others within the cramped ambit of their ideology. This, though, should not lead us to abandon or fail to appreciate a nobler and highly valuable sense of tradition, one that is inspired by many Confucian writings. This finer sense of tradition recognizes that human beings and the traditions they follow are defined by and help to shape one another. To fail to recognize the true nature of traditions and the roles they play in our lives not only gives us a false view of ourselves as well as others—something we shall show at greater length and detail in the following chapters— but also can erode support for critical foundations of value. It would be absurd to denigrate tradition and advocate museums, reject tradition and embrace the classics, condemn tradition and cherish history.[17]

At its worst, a blindly anti-traditional attitude and view can produce the type of person whose main aim in life is deprecating what others have achieved and value. Few, if any, though, really live in light of such a thorough rejection of tradition. Those who espouse such dramatic rhetoric still value many things; above all they are passionately devoted to their chosen lifestyle. The insistence on rejecting tradition traps them within a profound contradiction and leads them to seek an extremely odd future. If they are successful in getting everyone to join their cause, if they achieve their goal of eliminating traditions and shared values, they will no longer have a cause and a goal toward which to work; they will have succeeded in sawing off the limb upon which they stand. The truth is they need traditions to give meaning and direction even to the negative and narrow ends of their chosen lives.[18]

As noted above, part of understanding and living a life committed to tradition in the good sense that we are advocating requires appreciating the role that teachers play in maintaining and passing down traditions. Modern societies tend to overvalue and romanticize the great and extremely rare geniuses, those who enhance or transform a tradition in some profound way, and ignore those who exercise, pass on, keep alive, and invigorate—those like Kongzi who *transmit rather than create*—the traditions that produce such splendid individuals.[19] While highly creative individuals indeed are worthy of our respect and admiration, they are not by any means the whole story and should not lead us to ignore or undervalue other dimensions of achievement, meaning, and significance in human life. This is another way in which a proper sense of tradition can help us maintain a balanced and healthy view of what is important. Recognizing the central role of tradition allows us to see creative geniuses for what they are: not odd creatures who stand completely apart from human society and culture—who *transcend* humanity in the strong sense described above—but remarkable brothers and sisters, people who help to reshape, refine, and enhance our traditions: be they mathematical, musical, ethical, political, or spiritual. The modern, popular conception of the isolated genius not only offers a less accurate and complete understanding of how things work in the world, it can lead us to ignore the importance of the everyday and to forget that the exceptional arises out of this shared and more familiar soil. Such a mistaken view can result in a failure to recognize, applaud, and be grateful for the role that traditions and teachers play. It also casts some of the very best among us out of the human community that is their home; it can lead both these highly gifted individuals and the rest of us to undermine rather than to embrace our common humanity.

One extreme form of an anti-traditional view of the world finds expression in an idea that should repel more than attract us: the "self-made man." What could this express aside from a profound ignorance of biology and a disturbing delusion about the true source and spring of our greatest accomplishments? Such a view leads us to false and harmful beliefs and attitudes about what we can legitimately claim as our own. If we ignore the support, nurturance, and inspiration that every successful human being enjoys, we can forget all those who contributed to our achievements and neglect all the advantages society has afforded us along the way.[20] We can end up isolated, alienated, and sadly ungrateful for all that we have achieved and enjoy. We don't admire Newton any less because, as he put it, he was "standing on the shoulders of Giants."[21] Recognizing that none of us is self-made does not diminish the honor or achievements of the most gifted among us; to the contrary, as Xunzi and other Confucians have argued so persuasively and elegantly, it enhances and deepens the luster of their accomplishments by setting them within their true and proper frame and making clear the great benefits they bestow upon all of humanity.

Throughout the ages, philosophers have suggested different defining characteristics for what it is to be human. Examples include capacities such as reason, emotions such as empathy, or skills like the ability to make tools. While these surely are important parts of what make us human, just as clearly these are not *uniquely* human characteristics. Other creatures display all of these abilities, though admittedly not in the remarkably complex and diverse ways we do. If we seek not just a unique ability but ask also what enables us to achieve the complicated and variegated forms of life that we live, the best answer perhaps is our traditions.[22] Having, following, challenging, enhancing, and revering traditions has nothing to do with succumbing to a mind-numbing, creativity-constricting traditionalism; conceived of and practiced in the right ways, traditions describe the distinctive and unique form of human life. To deny or distance ourselves from our received traditions is to alienate ourselves from our contemporaries, turn away from our predecessors, lose touch with our ancestors, squander our inheritance, neglect our posterity, and remain blind to what is most characteristic about us as a species. The questions that should occupy us are not so much whether we will be parts of traditions but which ones we should support, what we owe and will contribute to them, and how we will leave them for those who are to follow.

2

CONCEPTIONS OF SELF, SOCIETY, AND WORLD

In general, for most of history, philosophers in the Western tradition have accepted the idea that the task of pursuing one's own good closely coheres and is inextricably intertwined with the task of working for the common good of society and fulfilling one's proper role in the great chain of being. According to a widely held notion of natural law, one's own good and what is right track and, in the long run, coincide with one another. On the basis of this happy congruence of welfare, every well informed and sensible person could find solid justification and motivation to do what is right. Properly understood, doing the *right* thing is *good* for you; it conduces to your own best interest, one cannot gain by doing wrong, and working for your own welfare serves the greater good as well. One of the marks of modern society as well as modern ethical theory is the unraveling of this presupposition.[1]

The first person to challenge the abiding faith in such a congruence of welfare was Hugo Grotius (1583–1645), who, in his masterpiece *The Laws of War and Peace*, argued that consistently doing what is just is simply foolish, since such a course of action clearly and regularly conflicts with and undermines one's own best interests.[2] Today it strikes many as abundantly clear that doing what is right or working for the common good often not only are not in one's best interests but clearly conflict with one's best interests. No matter how creatively one conceives of or finesses the notion of *self-interest*, no matter how *enlightened* a conception of it one employs, it seems it cannot bridge the gap between one's own and the greater good. This is what lies behind the commonly accepted view that doing what is right almost always involves a sacrifice and therefore is difficult and often unpleasant. Thus, the central problem that drove and still largely informs much of modern Western ethical theory is how to cut the Grotian Knot: how to reconcile doing what is right with the rational pursuit of one's own good.

This tension between the good of self and society or the world at large gained even greater force as more people be-came convinced—under the influence of Freud and largely mis-taken readings of Darwin—that human nature is fundamentally and often insidiously egocentric and that their *real* interests are exclusively or primarily material in nature.[3] Significant sacrifice will often seem irrational if not unintelligible to those seeking to maximize their own material self-interest. From such a perspec-tive, those who live for the sake of others seem to be in the grip of myth or delusion or manifesting some sad pathology; those who willingly sacrifice themselves for a cause or principle seem deeply confused and drifting perilously close to if not entering the camp of "fanatics." This has led modern ethicists to propose a variety of different theories that seek to reweave the moral fabric: to address the apparent fact that one's own good and the good of society sometimes pull in opposite directions and cannot be reconciled.[4] On the one hand we find the self and its interests; pursuing these exclusively or to excess leads us to act selfishly. On the other hand are society and the rest of the world—the needs and interests of other people, creatures, and things. We can dedicate our lives to the good of society or the world and act altruistically or "selflessly," though this sets a very high standard for ethical conduct. The alternative, which has in general become accepted as the right and reasonable thing to do, is to bemoan *sotto voce*—never blame—people for choosing to do much less. Almost no contemporary philosopher thinks we have a *duty* to be self-sacrificing Bodhisattvas or saints.[5] Morality should not be so stringent or demanding.[6] The most that moral or political theory can require of us is that we reign in or control our worst tendencies so that we avoid harming others in our personal search for satisfaction, fulfillment, and happiness, however one might conceive of these.

Some philosophers have noted and developed the idea that the single-minded pursuit of one's own happiness or pleasure leads to a kind of paradox or at least a deep and unavoidable tension in pursuit of one's practical goals: the *paradox of hedonism*. It seems that directly seeking one's own happiness leads one to a less happy life.[7] A person seeking to make her life as happy as it can possibly be will tend to focus on her personal welfare; her primary concern will be that her own life goes well. She will seek to accumulate as much as she can for herself and lose neither resources nor sleep with concerns about the welfare of others. This is roughly how Scrooge lived before his conversion to a more loving and generous life in Charles Dickens's well-known and beloved work *A Christmas Carol*.[8] Scrooge comes to see, in the course of the story, that his initial form of life is most unfulfilling: the best kinds of life require one to be actively and sincerely committed to the well-being of *other* people, creatures, and things. A good life entails focusing on the welfare of others and indeed such concern is part of what *constitutes* the goodness or happiness of such a life. We, and those around us, take more satisfaction and joy and find greater fulfillment in being and working for not only our own good or happiness but also the good and happiness of the world. In order, though, to seriously and sincerely take up the interests of others, one must put less emphasis upon oneself, to the point of being willing to sacrifice, at least on occasion, one's own well-being or happiness. It appears that one best serves the self by sacrificing the self!

Some think that this apparent problem can be avoided by starting out with a more self-centered view but then deemphasizing, effacing, and eventually forgetting this perspective in one's day-to-day judgments about what to do and what to value. On such a view, I might start out as Scrooge—excessively seeking to improve my personal welfare—but when I realize that it is in my own best interest to be concerned about others I will set out to ignore and forget my original self-centered perspective and eventually efface it from my heart and mind. Precisely how one is to do this is never worked out very carefully, and this illustrates a general lack in modern Western philosophy of a concern for the education of children, the details of self-cultivation, or the complexities of psychology. Nevertheless, the possibility of making such a transformation and understanding how one could do so are fundamentally important, for such a view and for ethics in general. Without careful and compelling explorations of such issues, the plausibility of such theories as reliable normative guides for action is greatly reduced. On the face of things, it seems at best odd to think we can lose sight of our egocentric perspective on the world, that we can become selfless *because* we see that it is to our advantage to be less self-centered, especially when such self-centered concern is described as the *very nature* of the self.

Other philosophers have raised some serious objections to the idea of bringing about such a change in one's point of view and orientation toward to the world. They argue that trying to efface one's self-interested perspective leads to a kind of "schizophrenia" within the self: on the one hand, purportedly, one ultimately or furtively values one set of concerns (one's own selfish interests); on the other, one practically and actively values or is motivated by something else (the well-being of others).[9] It is difficult to see how one can avoid profound and fundamental conflicts between these two evaluative schemes, not only in terms of how one justifies the ways in which one and others act but also and more severely in terms of motivating oneself and others to act in one way rather than another. Moreover, such an account just does not ring true to human experience. The self-effacing strategy does not capture what happens to Scrooge in the course of *A Christmas Carol*. His initial selfishness most definitely is not *what leads him*, at least not in any direct and discursive way, to expand the scope of his concern;

his change of heart is not the result of more clever self-interested calculation. In the course of the story, he comes to remember and realize that he in fact cares for other people and takes profound satisfaction and joy in their faring well. He comes to recognize his former overly self-centered perspective as not only flawed but shameful: something for which he works to make amends, seeks forgiveness, and hopes for redemption. The self-centered perspective neither justifies his new view about how he and others should act nor does it in any way explain or motivate his actions. His old way of life no longer has any appeal for or pull upon him at all, but he does not *forget* it or what it was like to live like that; his former life serves as a source of regret, a lesson learned, and a goad to be better. Scrooge is not employing a clever, effaced, self-interested perspective, the aim of which is to increase his welfare; he has taken up a different evaluative stance altogether, a different form of life. The story is not about a *shift in strategy* but a transformation of character, what is aptly described as a spiritual transformation or conversion. Scrooge is not the same man he was before; he is a "changed" man, a *better* man.

Confucianism, as well as other virtue-ethical traditions, may well offer a way out of this nettle of problems and paradoxes by relying upon and advocating a very different, more relational view of the self and sophisticated views about self-cultivation. The Confucian conception of the self—which describes human beings as integrally related to and to some degree defined by their connections with others—offers a significant contrast to many modern philosophical and psychological assumptions about agents as highly individuated, self-interested, calculating egos. Another important difference is that the Confucian model sees the ideal self as developing over the course of human life. We are not hard-surfaced impenetrable billiard balls following fixed and unchanging vectors of desire, destined to collide with and ricochet off one another; if we follow the Way, it can lead us to alter our constitution: to change, to improve, to transform ourselves.

The Confucian relational view of the self, like many other East Asian models of the self, often is misunderstood as describing or requiring a "loss" of self, which seems to advocate a plunge into oblivion or nihilism, possibilities that are alien, frightening, and wholly unappealing to most people's common sense—East or West. In contrast, the view I am describing is properly understood as presenting a way to gain an *expanded* conception of one's self and a greater sense of meaning in and for one's life. It offers the opportunity to take up and pursue a process of self-cultivation and personal transformation in a clear-eyed as opposed to a self-effacing or self-deceptive manner: whether one is looking forward, to the future, or back, over the course of one's life, one can recognize and endorse the changes this process entails. Indeed, such prospective previews and retrospective reviews are important parts of what keeps one moving forward and assures that one is and remains on the Way.

Such a life offers a way to fulfill a deep human need to find a greater and more meaningful sense of self, a need to be connected not only to other people and creatures but to the world at large: something grand and much greater than any individual self ever could be. The view is not that people cannot live decent lives without completely giving themselves over to the project of attaining the most expansive view of themselves possible but rather that a more expansive sense of oneself and one's many connections to the world makes eminently good sense and are parts of what makes life worth living: there is nothing irrational, mystical, or mysterious in not seeking to live for and by oneself. To the contrary, such a life recognizes and takes into account the undeniable fact of our many complex connections to the people, creatures, and things of the world and may well offer one of the most secure and appealing ways to live one's life.

The Confucian view of the self offers a sensible way out of the apparent paradox noted earlier by pointing out that while all of us begin life inclined to pursue our own interests and happiness— anyone who has cared for very young children knows this—we also begin life embedded in relationships that intimately connect our well-being—both materially and psychologically—with the good of others. Children naturally love and value the welfare of those who care for them and the good of a child's caretaker is an essential part not only of the child's happiness, but also of its sense of self. This is part of the legacy bequeathed to us by natural selection; without such dispositions, human beings would not have possessed the critical inclinations and capacities to form and sustain the relationships, groups, institutions, communities, and traditions that have enabled them not only to survive but to flourish.

Most philosophers who discuss the role of evolution in human ethics note the importance of "cooperation" to human survival. This is an important point but often the sense of co-operation in play is restricted to individual, one-off acts be-tween particular, independent "agents"—what we might call simple transactions—rather than temporally extended projects, relationships, communities, and traditions. Such a perspective presents human beings as if they began their lives as mature isolated individuals who then plan and live their lives by choos-ing, on a case-by-case or policy basis, to cooperate based on a *strategy* designed to maximize their individual well-being. As an account of how early humans lived together and evolved, this is wildly implausible; it leaves out critically important features of human biology, anthropology, psychology, and history and offers a misleading and artificially perplexing picture of contemporary human life.

Contrary to what vulgar and mistaken accounts of natural selection would lead one to believe, evolution has disposed us favorably toward many aspects of the world; we are not hostile, cold, or indifferent to the fate of much of what lives or merely exists around us; we are not inclined to see each and every thing simply as a means to the satisfaction of our immediate material or psychological needs or every other creature as a competitor in an unending zero-sum game or fight for survival. We value the world in varied and complex ways and have innate inclinations to be curious about, seek to understand, and relate ourselves to the world around us.[10] Most human beings who wholly lacked such inclinations simply did not survive; they did not possess the basic orientations and inclinations needed for creatures such as ourselves—who individually are weak and easy prey—to survive, understand, and master the world around them.

Confucians argue that we need to build on this natural state of relationship and affection and, through a process of self-cultivation, move from the more self-centered and self-interested stance to a genuinely ethical point of view. In a similar way, some modern environmentalists argue that we need to recognize, nurture, and come to appreciate our complex relationships with the world around us; this process will lead us to value the world more deeply, but it will also and at the same time lead us to feel more at home and fulfilled living within it. In either case, the process of cultivating the self does not lead one to "forget" or "efface" one's original stance; rather, one begins life with a richer palette of desires, including a variety of active concerns for other people, creatures, and things, and extends, expands, and transforms these, coming to regard any narrowly self-interested posture toward the world as incomplete, immature, and unappealing. The narrowly self-centered perspective loses its grip upon one as one takes up and embraces a broader view of the world and a more satisfying way to live within it. This process is sketched out in a passage that offers Kongzi's own spiritual autobiography:

> At fifteen, I committed myself to learning.
> At thirty, I stood firm.
> At forty, I had no doubts.
> At fifty, I understood the decree of Heaven.
> At sixty, my ear was attuned.
> At seventy, I followed my heart's desires without
>   over-stepping propriety. (*Analects* 2.4).

In the process of this fifty-five-year-long course of development or cultivation, Kongzi shaped himself in ways that no longer left his desires in conflict with what goodness demands. Rather than seeing this in terms of him finding clever ways to increase or monopolize the resources available to him, controlling or denying his "real" self-centered desires, effacing this perspective from his heart or consciousness, or paring away or losing these desires and thereby his "real" self, we should understand him as having developed a set of desires that led him to feel satisfaction, contentment, and joy with a certain moral mode of being in the world. When he started out on the path that produced this transformation he could look forward in a clear-eyed way to a better life than he had, one, though, that he only understood imperfectly. When successful and advanced along the path of the Way, he could look back upon his choice not only with no regrets about having chosen it but also with a sense of relief and gratitude for having found and followed the Way. Nothing like self-effacement or self-deception is needed to follow the Way; it produces no schizophrenia within the self. Rather, it results in a sense of what Aristotle called "flourishing" (*eudaimonia*) or "blessedness" (*makaria*) or what Kongzi, as in the passage quoted above, called "understanding the decree of Heaven" (知天命), and it brings with it a special and particularly satisfying sense of joy (*le* 樂).[11]

In the early stages of the tradition, the Confucian way of understanding the self and the good life was described through two primary sets of metaphors or two conflicting and competing theories about human nature. One of Kongzi's earliest followers, Mengzi 孟子 (391–308 BCE), developed a set of agricultural metaphors that cast human self-cultivation in terms of natural growth and development.[12] On such a view, human beings are born with tender ethical "sprouts" (*duan* 端) of virtue, which if properly tended, develop into strong and vibrant critical dispositions.

> A sense of concern and commiseration is the sprout of benevolence.
> A sense of shame and dislike is the sprout of righteousness.
> A sense of yielding and deference is the sprout of ritual propriety.
> A sense of approval and disapproval is the sprout of wisdom...

> We all have these four sprouts within us. Know that we
>   simply must
> extend and fill them out, and they shall be like a fire begin-
>   ning to burn,
> or a spring pushing up through [the ground]. (*Mengzi* 2A6)

Slightly later, another follower of the Confucian way, Xunzi 荀子 (310–219 BCE), explicitly argued against Mengzi's interpretation of the master's teachings and insisted that self-cultivation is largely a humanly designed, artificial regimen of shaping, sharpening, and polishing.[13] We chisel, cut, file, and polish our characters out of a rough and unruly original nature, which Xunzi variously likened to an unshaped hunk of metal, lump of clay, or crooked timber. Xunzi quoted with approval some lines from the *Book of Odes* (*Shijing* 詩經), which Kongzi himself had quoted earlier as an illustration of the process of self-cultivation,[14] "As we cut and chisel, as we file and polish" (如切如磋如琢如磨). Along with Xunzi's rich assortment of related craft metaphors and analogies, these lines clearly capture and express his general views about human nature and the process of self-cultivation.[15]

Regardless of which of these interpretations one follows—and the most adequate account is almost certainly a judicious com- bination of the two—one finds on either model that the process of Confucian self-cultivation shares several significant features in common. First, Mengzi and Xunzi both insist that human atten- tion and effort are needed to develop human nature from its early, natural state to ethical excellence. While some modern commen- tators describe Mengzi as employing "vegetative" metaphors to describe the process of self-cultivation, this is inaccurate and quite misleading.[16] Self-cultivation is not a wholly spontaneous, undi- rected, or uncontrolled activity. Mengzi's primary metaphors are *agricultural*. They portray self-cultivation as a distinctively *human* activity, requiring elevated levels of sustained attention, reflec- tion, care, and effort, as well as a proper environment and timely rain and sunshine, in order to bring it to completion. Agricultural production is part of a long and still ongoing *tradition* of human endeavor, and this fact must not be lost in presenting an interpretation of Mengzi's views. Nor should we forget that it was the invention of agriculture, some ten thousand years ago, that created the possibility of large settled civilizations and their cultures. In at least this respect, the practice that gave rise to modern life in all its variety and complexity, like the cultures that it generated, is an intricate combination of nature and invention. The Confucian Way is not *wholly* natural any more than agriculture is; both distill the best results of a long process of experience, reflection, experimentation and critical refinement and urge us to follow this accumulated wisdom as our guide in life.[17] Some Western thinkers allow for transformations of self, but very few describe so profound or thoroughgoing a transformation as the Confucians advocate and none of course embraces the particular assumptions or prescribes the approaches and aims of Confucianism.

Xunzi's more craft-oriented metaphors share all of these features. Self-cultivation does not just "happen"; it requires a great deal of sustained awareness, attention, reflection, and personal effort and depends in important ways on being in, maintaining, and making the most of the right kind of environment. Second, while Mengzi and Xunzi place greater or less emphasis on the role of tradition, ritual, and teachers, both agree that these are critical resources for successful self-cultivation. Mengzi's agricultural metaphors no less than Xunzi's craft metaphors imply that the work of self-cultivation is a long and challenging regimen involving dedicated study, practice, attentiveness, and reflection. Third, and most important in regard to our present set of concerns, both these early Confucians saw self-cultivation as aimed at producing a fundamental *transformation* of the self. Whether that transformation is inspired and illustrated by drawing analogies to the cultivation and maturation of plants or in terms of manufacturing knives, vases, and wheels out of raw minerals, clay, and wood the point is unmistakably the same. Those who successfully move from the uncultivated state to the state of culture and character that define the Confucian ideal become different, *better* people. They have new desires and motivations, new concerns and aims, and new practices and policies. As Kongzi did in the course of his own life, they move from being people who *want to be good*, to people who reliably are and are at peace in the good.

Mengzi's agricultural metaphors for self-cultivation as well as Xunzi's craft-inspired analogies both show that moral cultivation not only requires sustained and concerted personal effort but also relies upon a critically constructed and time-tested social background of attitudes, norms, practices, and institutions. Here we see the complex interconnection between human nature's capacities and society's supporting structures, between nature and nurture, or genes and culture. Ethics relies upon human nature to describe what is possible and every moral theory describes or assumes related views about human nature and psychology.[18] Ethics also requires humanly fashioned cultures to provide both ethical ideals and standard means to achieve them. Self-cultivation, broadly construed, describes the process of these two working together. The social aspects of self-cultivation are evident in many of the topics explored in this volume: tradition, ritual, music, and so forth, but the general, social nature of ethics is equally on display in Confucian views about the self and how it is embedded within a complex of familial and social relationships. This relationship between self and society, an understanding of who one is and how one relates to other people, creatures, and things in the world, is essential not only for understanding Confucianism but also for appreciating some of the distinctive ways in which it can contribute to ethical theory in general.

We can get a fairly good sense of important aspects of the process of early Confucian moral self-cultivation by thinking of it as roughly analogous to what happens when people who have never been in good physical shape resolve to get into good physical shape and successfully commit themselves to a comprehensive regimen that changes not only their bodies but also their outlook upon and style of life. When such people start out, they are motivated mostly by dissatisfaction with aspects of their current life: they are often out of breath and tire easily; they can't engage in activities they would like to try; they are not happy with their physical appearance and perhaps dissatisfied with or ashamed of being unable to control their eating and drinking and their general lack of self-discipline. They know that their present style of life will almost surely shorten their lifespan and diminish the quality of whatever years they have left to live. At the same time, they look to people who are healthy and robust and see the possibility of eliminating or mitigating all or at least many of these dissatisfactions and concerns. They also are drawn to descriptions, offered by other people, of the special physical and psychological goods associated with having a strong and healthy body and a disciplined life, which of course includes the good regard of other people, as well as their own imagined experiences of these goods. All these give them sound and persuasive reasons to take up and pursue a regimen of physical training. If, like Kongzi, they successfully follow the course to which they have committed themselves, they will enjoy a range of benefits, some of which they understood only dimly when they first set out upon this way. Just as they were able to set out with good reasons, they will be able to look back and feel satisfaction at having chosen and done well. They will feel they are living a different and better kind of life; they will feel they are flourishing, they are fortunate, perhaps even that they are blessed, and that they are making full use of their natural abilities and talents. They may feel they understand and are living in accord with the decree of Heaven; in any event, they will experience the special sense of satisfaction and joy that comes to all who succeed in following and finding a better way to live.

Following the Way does not require people to attempt to efface a clever, self-serving strategy in order to realize a better way of life. Confucian moral self-cultivation describes a gradual and progressive process of transformation in the course of which one extends and augments an overly self-centered conception of oneself in order to arrive at a more expansive sense of oneself; one comes to see oneself as intricately and extensively connected with and committed to the welfare of other people, creatures, and things. Rather than losing any clear sense of oneself and falling into a dark selfless night of oblivion, one develops and enjoys an enlarged conception of oneself and a clearer and more secure sense of one's place in the world. This grander perspective and more comprehensive sense of oneself and one's relationship to the rest of the world leads one naturally to aim not only at one's own narrow, self-centered welfare and happiness but also the welfare and happiness of other people, creatures, and things.[19] The process of losing an earlier more constricted self gives rise to the peace, satisfaction, fulfillment, and joy of the cultivated Confucian and offers a model and ideal that remains as attractive today as it has proven to be for more than two millennia.

3

SOCIAL PRACTICES
GREAT AND SMALL

Confucians have shown a deep, sustained, and revealing concern with "ritual" (*li*) and its potential to produce and exert a range of effects—some subtle, some profound—on human life; their views have much to teach us about how such shared, traditional behaviors shape, direct, enliven, and give meaning and tempo to the ways in which we and others live.[1] My general aim in this chapter is to argue that social rituals play a critical and vastly underappreciated role in our lives and are especially important for living more humane lives together. I will make my case by introducing some traditional Confucian views about ritual and suggesting ways in which such ideas still do or should play a role in contemporary cultures.

The sense of Confucian *li* is much broader than our word "ritual," including not only august religious ceremonies but also everyday conventions and norms of meeting, greeting, leave-taking, and the like. As is true in the case of what qualifies as a tradition, it is not always clear when a shared practice should be thought of as a ritual. Practices that are trivial or merely passing fashion clearly do not qualify as rituals in the requisite sense, but some fairly common practices, such as the Western custom of shaking hands when meeting or parting, surely are rituals.[2] Hand shaking is a good example of a ritual the true significance of which often is lost in familiarity and routine and shows that thinking about such practices in terms of their ritual value can be a revealing way to reflect upon our lives. Here too there is a parallel with tradition; both rituals and tradition are core features of a Confucian point of view.

Confucian *li* includes those regular, stylized social practices that express significance or meaning beyond their instrumental utility, those behaviors that possess symbolic value to those within a shared community. In our time and society, people practice rituals in many diverse contexts. Baptisms, Bar and Bat Mitzvahs, weddings, funerals, graduations, the swearing in of a new president or Supreme Court justice, the opening of Congress, the start of most sporting events, or presenting a paper at an academic conference are just some of the common occasions for ritual practice in contemporary American society. Celebrations such as baby showers would fall within the scope of modern Confucian ritual, and in light of the importance of giving birth to and raising children, such events arguably should be accorded greater recognition and value than they commonly command. Such shared social celebrations often are examples of an implicit or latent ritual that should be embraced in a more explicit and manifest way. In between the grand and more modest examples of ritual are a wide range of shared social practices some of which qualify as rituals in our sense of the word and others which might not. For example, singing the national anthem at the start of a baseball game clearly qualifies as a ritual, as does the president throwing out the first pitch of the season, but the way players shake hands before most sporting events or the "ceremonial coin toss" at the start of football games to determine which team kicks off and which receives also are examples of rituals in the Confucian sense. Kongzi took all rituals—great and small—very seriously, because of their expressive and symbolic importance and their ability to connect us not only to each other but to those who preceded us and who will follow us as well. Kongzi also valued rituals because they called on him and others to work on themselves, to cultivate the proper sense of reverence and emotion appropriate on such occasions. The greatest rituals offered an inexhaustible source of meaning and inspiration.

> Someone asked for an explanation of the sacrifice to the
>   imperial ancestors.
> The master said, "I cannot fully explain it, wouldn't
>   anyone who *could* explain it see everything in the world
>   as clearly as looking here?" (pointing to the palm of his
>   hand) (*Analects* 3.11)

The scope of Confucian ritual is interwoven with and extends even farther into the fabric of social life than the examples enumerated above might suggest; Kongzi thought the clothes we wear and how we maintain and wear them, our deportment and demeanor, how we sit upon our mats and whether our mats are properly arranged, what food we eat and how we cut and consume it—all these things fall within the ambit of ritual. Kongzi saw that all of these activities can be important; all can both express to others how we think about ourselves and the world around us, all can exert an influence upon those we meet and interact with, and all can serve as means to cultivate ourselves in ways that contribute to a more humane social ideal. While many contemporary people would initially dismiss the idea, the truth is that our clothing *does* matter and how we care for and wear our clothes matters too. We recognize this in many ways; for example, on "formal" occasions, having the appropriate clothes in good condition, wearing them properly, and carrying oneself in an appropriate manner all are important: these are ways we express the solemnity and seriousness of important occasions. It would be not only inappropriate but disrespectful and callous to come to the funeral of a friend's mother wearing mud-stained shorts, sandals, and a happy-face t-shirt. In addition to expressing and symbolizing the appropriate orientation and attitude, the effort we put into procuring the proper clothing, wearing it properly, and holding ourselves in a dignified manner all work *on us*; these things can help to put us in the proper state of mind, whether it be a sad and solemn occasion such as a funeral or a happy event like celebrating the fiftieth anniversary of one's parents' marriage. Isn't much the same thing true when we go to meet someone for a date or go out with our spouse for dinner? Don't we make special efforts to present ourselves in a certain way, and isn't this effort aimed at both putting ourselves in the proper frame of mind, expressing what is in our hearts, communicating it clearly to the one we care for, and displaying it to the rest of the world?[3] This is the core sense and sensibility of Confucian ritual, and it can function in equally powerful and important ways on ordinary as well as extraordinary occasions.

Charles Taylor has done a brilliant job showing how the rich and complex phenomena of human language enable us to express, develop, and continue to interpret who and what we are; he has shown that language is one of the primary means through which we cultivate the understanding, stance, and attitudes that constitute our sense of ourselves and others.[4] It is helpful to think of Confucian ritual as a somatic or kinetic form of language: a set of cultural norms and practices that allows us to understand, express, develop, and continue to interpret who and what we are, and that gives concrete shape to our forms of life. Like language, rituals have a grammar that structures and informs what particular behaviors mean, how they go together and relate to other aspects of culture and individual action. A ceremony has an opening, middle, and conclusion designed to bring practitioners from their everyday world to a new and more profound relationship with the world, and then return them to normal life, often restored, strengthened, reinvigorated, and inspired. Individual ritual acts and gestures have particular senses and in this way are like the semantic component of a natural language. Finally, ritual performances can be done in different manners or styles which, like styles of speech, add sense and nuance to what is expressed and communicated.[5] Indeed language, often a special kind of language, is part of and works together with most rituals to achieve their various ends. Both these phenomena regularly are parts of and work together with music as well, as we shall explore more fully in the following chapter. These connections explain why Kongzi was deeply concerned about language, as well as ritual and music, and wanted to ensure that language not only properly reflected but also influenced the shape, rhythm, and aims of our social world.

> The Master said, ". . . If names are not correct, speech will not go smoothly. If speech does not go smoothly, endeavors will not be successful. If endeavors are not successful, rituals and music will not flourish. If rituals and music do not flourish, punishments and penalties will not be appropriate. If punishments and penalties are not appropriate, the people will not know where to place hand or foot!" (*Analects* 13.3)

Many modern people, and perhaps most in the West, regard ritual as a fulsome or at best quaint remnant of a backward age or something appropriate only for solemn religious occasions. Many of the same people consider both language and music to be ways for individuals to express personal opinions, preferences, or feelings and largely a matter of taste; these aspects of our lives are not thought to bear directly on weighty matters like politics and ethics. Surely, though, ritual, language, and music play major roles in these more communal aspects of life, which in turn has direct and profound consequences for each and every individual. I argued for the importance of tradition in chapter one and will make a similar case in chapter four in regard to music; here I endeavor to defend such a view about ritual and language.

In chapter one, I suggested that human language itself constitutes a kind of tradition; we could add that, contrary to what many people believe, human languages are fundamentally *social*, not personal, activities. As Ludwig Wittgenstein demonstrated, the very concept of a language entails that it is shared and public; a private language, in the sense of one that others *could not* in principle share, simply is not possible.[6] In nature and function, languages are shared ways of referring and responding to the world, of expressing, discussing, performing, and continually modifying and honing our ability to understand, communicate, and coordinate our actions with others. The remarkable power of language to shape our perception of the world and our responses to it testifies to its fundamentally social, political, and ethical dimensions, and these aspects of language are on display in almost every social, political, or ethical controversy.[7]

Like ritual, language plays a subtle yet powerful role in the formation of our attitudes and values. Take a young person who is taught and regularly employs racist, misogynist, or homophobic language. Such a person learns to refer to and think about certain other human beings in terms of categories that mark them as inherently lacking many of the qualities that make human beings and human relationships valuable. They are taught to see these other people—their brothers and sisters in humanity—as fundamentally different from and inferior to themselves and their favored in-group and are encouraged to take pride and delight in their alleged superiority. It is clear that in such cases language shapes not only their views of certain others, but their understanding of themselves as well. Even this brief example reveals some of the ways in which language works to form and focus important attitudes and beliefs. A person taught such language comes to the world oriented to see, hear, and respond in characteristic ways: ways that are racist, misogynist, or homophobic. Being shaped, oriented, and inclined in these ways by language, it is no simple matter to disabuse such people of their sadly false and despicable attitudes and beliefs; they dwell within a form of life that conspires to keep them within its bent and twisted ambit, which pushes and pulls them to interpret the phenomena they encounter in ways that cohere and reinforce this particular stance on the world. This is true for other, less odious ways of seeing the world as well and shows that behind parental advice to "not use that kind of language" or even "that tone of voice" lie deep and important lessons. Kongzi was concerned with even subtle nuances of expression.

> [The disciple] Zi Xia asked about filial piety.
> The Master said, "The difficult thing is the look on one's face. If when there is something that needs to be done, the young take upon themselves the difficult work or when there is food and wine, the elders are served first, is this all there is to filial piety?" (*Analects* 2.8)

It is commonly thought that learning is primarily a matter of taking in and processing information that we receive through written or spoken language. Language does of course play a remarkable role in helping us to understand the world around us, but the role it plays is much more complex than this simple description implies. Many important lessons require not only cognitive but affective and somatic understanding: we must not only process information but also appreciate and respond to actions and states of affairs.[8] We often understand and respond to other people by spontaneously empathizing with or simulating their behavior; we have evolved to mimic a range of behaviors and are primed to respond to certain gestures, movements, and postures, some of which are quite subtle and often go largely unnoticed. In all such cases, language per se plays no direct role in how we come to understand.

The practice of rituals is another way of learning and a good example of how complex the process of learning certain lessons can be. We can begin the practice of a ritual with little cognitive or emotional sense of what the ritual is meant to express or convey. Confucians, as well as others, recognize that ritual *practice* often precedes proper feeling or understanding in the process of cultivating ethical dispositions; in some cases, to a significant extent, the ritual itself is at least partly constitutive of both proper feeling and cognitive understanding. As Brad Wilburn has argued, these three—practice, feeling, and understanding—usually take turns and cooperate in the development of virtue and the larger project of forming and defining a way of life.[9] As noted above, ritual practice can precede proper feelings or conceptual understanding, but this is not always the case. Sometimes we grasp the point first and engage in ritual in order to control, evoke, fill out, or shape our emotional dispositions; sometimes we are moved by a feeling, image, or symbol and as a result take up the practice of ritual, which leads us to greater and more precise understanding. The point is that knowing is extremely complex both as a process and a state and often rituals of various types play a critical and largely unappreciated role.

In the remaining part of this chapter, I would like to explore how a ritually sensitive and informed perspective on the world, inspired by the Confucian tradition, can help us to become more aware of and attentive to important yet neglected aspects of contemporary life. I will first review some of the many rituals that inform, embellish, and enliven our modern lives and discuss some areas in modern life that lack but call out for ritual. I then will discuss in greater detail rituals of greeting and leave-taking in different cultures and argue that those of traditional China are at least as good and can be seen as superior in a number of respects to the rituals followed in the West. Part of my argument here includes a recommendation that contemporary Chinese people seriously consider setting aside or at least augmenting the Western rituals they currently practice and work to revive their tradition's forms of greeting and leave-taking. I will conclude with a final plea for greater attention to ritual and defend the idea that we are responsible morally for the rituals that inform, direct, and give shape to our lives.

As I noted earlier, we tend to think of rituals only in the context of grand rites of passage, events such as graduations, inaugurations, marriages, and funerals; few will gainsay the role such ceremonies play in the course of human life. The importance of the events such major rituals mark tends to overshadow the significance of minor, daily rituals, but in fact the latter make up a much larger proportion of our lives and contribute more to our attitudes, dispositions, beliefs, actions, and overall sense of ourselves, others, and the lives we lead. In the opening sections of this chapter, I made reference to a number of rituals observed in sports, and I would like to return to this topic in order to explore it at greater length and in more detail.

The meaning of participation in sports has changed in the course of history, but one feature remains especially important for our purposes: the role sports plays in the cultivation of a sense of justice or fairness. John Rawls's celebrated work *A Theory of Justice*,[10] the most influential account of justice in the twentieth century, conceives of justice in terms of fairness. Although many who defend Rawls's view fail to pay attention to the latter parts of his splendid book, Rawls spends a good deal of time there discussing the importance of a *sense* of justice and its possible origins.[11] I would like to suggest that one of the most important sources of a sense of justice as fairness is certain ritual aspects of playing sports.[12] Much of what I say applies equally well to play or games in general, but sports involve physical competition, which makes the importance of fairness more vivid and visceral, and unlike most other forms of play or games, the physicality of sports seem to necessitate rituals for encouraging fairness.[13] In many sports, it is common and accepted practice that competitors shake hands before competing in games in which they do everything they can to physically and psychologically dominate and defeat the other. Throughout the course of a competition, players must adhere to a set of rules that apply equally to all and that often are enforced by a special, disinterested group of third-party participants: referees.[14] When the final bell sounds or whistle blows one player or team is declared the winner. The norm then is for players to again shake hands, but even when sore feelings make this perfunctory or the ritual is omitted the losing team almost never *rejects* the decision. Just about the only time this occurs is when there is a clear and widely shared perception that the game has been less than *fair*. This should strike us as quite remarkable and for at least the following two reasons. First, it testifies to a profound commitment to fair play by not only the contestants but their fans or supporters as well. Second, this commitment is clearly a result of practice and custom rather than of learning or adhering to some theory of justice. Our sense of fairness finds one of its most important sources in largely unselfconscious social practices and norms regarding sports or what Confucians would understand as the rituals of competition. Kongzi explores this set of phenomena in the *Analects*.

> The master said, "Cultivated individuals never contend. [Perhaps someone will say] they must contend when they compete in ritual archery contests. On such occasions, though, they salute and defer [to the other competitors] when they take up their position and raise a glass to toast them, when they step down. In so contending, they remain cultivated individuals" (*Analects* 3.7).[15]

Modern technology has created the demand for new rituals but our current dim view of ritual has either failed to sustain new rituals when they have developed or, more recently, has failed to develop new rituals at all. The result has been more perplexity, uncertainty, and anxiety and the loss of a certain measure of humanity in our everyday social lives. The telephone is a good example of a technology that early on generated new social rituals that for the most part have not been sustained and that continues to call for additional ritual innovation. People used to initiate a phone conversation with a greeting and introduction: "Hello, this is Alexander G. Bell" or receive a call by saying "Hello, this is the Bell residence, Alexander speaking," to which the calling party would respond by declaring her name and explaining the reason for the call.[16] Nowadays, people often "answer" a call without saying anything or perhaps saying something that is more confusing than informative or inviting, like "Talk to me!" or "Yo!"[17] Many, though not all, of today's phones have digital caller ID, but a large percentage of calls are not made by or to people who know who we are. This technological advance poses new issues of etiquette, for there is no norm governing such things as whether one should answer or can ignore a call from someone one knows. The use of cell phones extends the range of such decisions, for now we can receive calls almost anywhere and at any time. Cell phones also *impose* our phone conversations on others and often constitute a considerable invasion of other peoples' personal space. Most airlines are attentive to the severity of this problem by banning cell phone conversations; who wants to hear the person next to them babbling on about intimate personal matters, inane chatter, or serious conversations throughout a long flight?[18] The ability to switch between callers and put some on hold poses additional challenges and often leads to offense and hurt feelings. Modern communicative technologies offer us some remarkable opportunities to stay in touch and share our thoughts and feelings with one another. Skype gives people separated by vast distances an almost magical ability to see and hear one another in a real-time environment. But some technologies work to separate and splinter us, at times dividing and isolating age groups from one another; consider how difficult it is for most parents to understand text messages sent by their own children.

This poses new and severe challenges to developing shared rituals.[19] The point in all of these cases is that without shared practices governing and guiding us in such matters, technology has created many more ways and opportunities not only to communicate but also to isolate, offend, and insult people, intentionally or not. E-mail raises many additional problems. Who knows whether it is impolite not to answer a given e-mail or what period of time can pass before one should answer? In this case too, the power of our rituals has failed to keep pace with the advance of our technology; the result is more efficient but less humane interactions.

I would now like to discuss briefly rituals of greeting and leave-taking in the West and China. Handshaking was practiced in the Mediterranean world as a gesture of greeting as least as early as the second century BCE, perhaps even earlier. Some argue handshaking was introduced to Europe by Sir Walter Raleigh during the sixteenth century and originated as a gesture of peace: extending one's empty, strong right hand showed that one neither carried nor concealed a weapon. Of course, the handshake is only one of many ritual ways of greeting and taking leave; others kiss cheeks or hands, hug, rub noses, tip hats, do the dap, high five, or bow to announce and express friendly greeting or farewell. Under normal conditions, contemporary Westerners expect people to shake with bare not gloved hands; appreciate a firm, not limp, grip; and assume people will look them in the eye and announce an appropriate greeting or farewell. Of course, like most rituals, the handshake allows for many subtle variations and accompanying gestures that alter what is communicated. The ritual of the handshake is so much a part of meeting and parting that it normally goes unnoticed, but rejecting the offer of a handshake still is considered extremely rude and deeply insulting. Handshakes fit in well with cultures of individuality: whatever its true origin, the physical act of shaking hands is a person-to-person gesture and carries with it the sense of two equals meeting in mutual recognition and acceptance.

Bowing has been practiced in many cultures throughout the world. In East Asia it takes many forms and can express a range of different attitudes or ideas including respect, admiration, apology, thanks, deference, humility, and greeting. I am interested in a form of greeting commonly employed in traditional China and still in use, though not as widely, among Chinese people today. This is a gesture of greeting and farewell that I will refer to as "salutation" (*yi* 揖). It is performed by cupping one hand over the other, raising both hands in front of one, and gently shaking them, roughly by rotating the joints of one's wrists and elbows, while bowing one's head. Typically, though not necessarily, this gesture is accompanied by a verbal greeting. Chinese salutation is a highly commendable way to greet people, and I hope the Chinese people will consider reviving this traditional form of greeting and farewell among them. Here are some reasons to value the social practice of salutation. First, from a public hygiene point of view, saluting someone is *much better* than shaking their hand.[20] Let's face it, when it comes to strangers and sometimes even people we know, it is not always a welcome thing to find oneself obliged to clasp their hand. You don't know where that hand has been recently, and in some cases, you *don't want* to know.[21] Chinese-style saluting is a much better alternative; it acknowledges that you are glad to see someone without committing you to share in their personal hygiene, such as it may be, or perhaps simply in the bad luck of what they have come in contact with. Second, saluting enables you to greet or say farewell to groups of people en masse. If you walk into a room full of people, you can salute them all and say "greetings to everyone" (大家好), and you can employ the same gesture when you take your leave. Handshaking would require having to engage each person individually, which often makes it impractical. It also requires you to choose who will be first and who last in your order of greeting or leave taking, something which in almost all cases is neither necessary nor welcome. In cases of en masse greeting or farewell, Westerners often substitute a wave to stand in for multiple handshakes. In any event, salutation is more amenable than handshaking alone to greeting or saying farewell to groups of people; in this respect, it is less bound to the perspective of individual, person-to-person interaction in strongly egalitarian societies.[22] For all these reasons, it is an admirable ritual, worthy of consideration, appreciation, and adoption.[23]

In light of all that has been said above about rituals, it should be clear why we are responsible for the rituals that are practiced in our society. We are responsible for the stance we take toward and the ways in which we interact with other people, creatures, and things; since ritual plays an important role not only in how we shape and express our view, orientation, and response to the world, we should be aware of, reflect on, evaluate, and when necessary reform or innovate rituals so that they achieve ideals we all endorse.[24] We see Kongzi engaged in such reflection on ritual practice in *Analects* 9.3.

> The master said, "A linen cap is prescribed by ritual. Nowadays, people wear a silk one. That is less expensive, and so I go along with the popular practice. Bowing before one ascends [the steps of the hall] is prescribed by ritual. Nowadays, people bow when they reach the top of the stairs. That is arrogant, and so, while it goes against popular practice, I bow before I ascend."

Kongzi did not follow or advocate traditionalism; he is willing to accommodate changes in ritual practice, but only if there is good reason to do so. He will not accept changes, even seemingly small ones, that harm or threaten the underlying justification for ritual, which is to fashion, practice, and maintain a more decent and meaningful form of human life.

For similar reasons, we should attend much more to the language that we use and develop a greater awareness and sensitivity to the ways in which language both expresses and shapes our values and affects those around us. We understand these issues on the large scale, for example great state ceremonies, and when it comes to dramatic effects, such as hate speech, but we draw too sharp and strict a boundary around such cases and ignore the degree to which everyday rituals and language matter in our daily lives. As we shall explore further in chapter six, Confucians call on us to become more aware of our traditions, rituals, language, music, and many other aspects of our lives—great *and* small—in light of the ways these express and shape who we are and how we affect the people, creatures, and things of the world. In the following chapter, we shall extend this argument for the need for greater awareness, sensitivity, and concern to the particular case of music.

4

MUSIC IN AND OF OUR LIVES

For most of us, music is thought to be a form of recreation, a means of personal enjoyment and relaxation; it is primarily a kind of diversion, largely considered a matter of individual taste, and as it often is said "there is no accounting for matters of taste" (*de gustibus non est disputandum*). Such, though, is not the case for professional musicians and others who have devoted themselves to music in one way or another, nor has this been the attitude toward or conception of music characteristic of most of the cultures on earth for most of history. And while most of us tend to *say* that preference in music is *simply* a matter of taste, many of us seem to take such preferences much more seriously than such a declaration suggests. To say of someone that they have bad or terrible taste in music seems to say something significant about them *as a person*.

For the greater part of human history and in many parts of the world today music has been and is regarded as much more important, an activity laden with meaning, power, and significance and closely related to the well-being of individuals, groups, institutions, and states. For many people, music is largely a spiritual enterprise. Even when it lacks an overtly spiritual dimension, it often is regarded as the primary vehicle and reservoir of cultural values and orientations.[1] Music often has been associated with specific observances or festivals and commonly accompanied by special rituals.

If we stop and think about it, these concerns are not wholly absent in our own contemporary culture. Most weddings still employ Mendelssohn's "Wedding March," one will hear Elgar's "Pomp and Circumstance" at graduation and the "Star Spangled Banner" is played and often sung at the start of baseball games and many other important social events. The military marks the death of soldiers with "Taps" and quickens their fighting spirit with martial music. Every branch of service maintains an official band, which often is on display in both military and civilian settings leading parades or supporting other forms of commemoration or celebration. In each of these cases, as well as others we shall explore below, people do not passively sit and listen to others playing music; often both performers and audience *move* in stylized ways in harmony with the music.

Martial music of a different sort encourages and incites the crowds at football games and many other sporting events; it is hard to imagine people watching such competitions without being roused by the characteristic music; the music provides a score for this and other types of human behavior that is as crucial as the sound track is for a movie. When people gather together to have fun, they often do so according to the rhythm and beat of "party music"; indeed, music of some kind seems to be an indispensable part of *any* party. In more intimate settings, certain kinds of music are thought to enhance and "set the mood" for romance; years later, people recall with joy and find deeply meaningful songs associated with such moments. Most couples have a particular, special song they regard as "our song"; consider, for example, the significance of "As Time Goes By" in the movie *Casablanca*.

Casablanca also includes a remarkably memorable and powerful scene in which music serves a purely political purpose. The Czech Resistance leader Victor Laszlo orders the house band at Rick's Café Américain to play the French national anthem, "La Marseillaise," in response to "The Watch on the Rhine" (*Die Wacht am Rhein*), a patriotic German song with origins rooted in older German conflicts with France, which was being sung by a group of Nazi soldiers. Laszlo starts singing "La Marseillaise" and soon long-suppressed patriotic emotions boil to the surface and erupt from the crowd; everyone joins in, drowning out the Germans and leading their embarrassed commander to insist that the club immediately be shut down. In all these cases, music plays serious and complex roles: it represents and sustains specific cultures, traditions, or points of view; it expresses or arouses certain emotions, it is associated with particular kinds of events or activities; it stimulates people to move along with its beat and rhythm and often is performed in the context of supporting rituals. In these circumstances, music is a much more weighty and significant matter; this was how it was regarded in ancient China.

Early Confucians taught that the songs the people of a state most enjoyed listening to and singing revealed deep and important things about their character, attitudes, and the future prospects of the state. One could tell if a ruler was succeeding or failing in his duties by reflecting upon the songs of his subjects. If their songs were joyful and happy, this showed they were contented and at ease and the king and his state were secure. If their songs were mournful and resentful, this manifested sadness and dissatisfaction and the king and his state were in jeopardy. In other words, music could be used as a *diagnostic* tool to gauge the mood of the people, the success of an administration, and the future prospects of a regime.[2] The idea that the music of different ages or states reflects the hearts and minds and general well-being of its people is summed up in a passage from the "Record of Music" (*Yueji* 樂記) chapter of the *Book of Rites*.[3]

> The music of a well ordered age is peaceful and joyful; its
>   government is harmonious. The music of a disordered
>   age is resentful and angry; its government is perverse.
>   The music of a state that is lost is mournful and anxious;
>   its people are hard-pressed.

The "Record of Music" does not even consider that there could be a society wholly *devoid of* music—and I suggest that we cannot easily imagine such a society—which reflects an underlying belief that music is an expression of basic and essential human urges, needs, inclinations, and aspirations and that it is a characteristic feature of human communities.[4] This is an important observation, both because it is true, and because it recognizes the profound importance of music in our lives. Many people wrongly think that music and other forms of art are dispensable—optional "extras" that somehow get added on to the *real* business of human life. In fact, music and other forms of art are no less and are arguably *much more* fundamental expressions of our distinctive nature than is a quality such as rationality. If you met someone who showed little ability for abstract, rational thought, you would be wise not hire him as a physicist or philosopher, but the thought that he was not human probably would not even occur to you. On the other hand, if you met someone who showed little or no interest in or ability for music or any other arts, who did not in any way adorn herself or decorate her surroundings or notice when others did such things, you might well begin to wonder what kind of creature was standing before you. We give voice to our joys and sorrows, regrets and aspirations as easily as we breathe; we adorn ourselves, decorate our environment, and express ourselves in a bewildering array of visual forms as naturally as we move our limbs and walk, in rhythm, upon the earth.

In addition to the diagnostic function of music described above and perhaps even more important to early Chinese thinkers was its *therapeutic* or *didactic* function. Kongzi and those who followed him believed that music had much to teach us and had great and subtle power to influence and shape our behavior, character, and lives. In *Analects* 8.8 Kongzi says, "Be stimulated by the odes; take your stand on the rites, and be perfected by music" (興於詩立於禮成於樂). These three: the poems of the *Book of Odes*, the traditional rites, and classical forms of music, were central components of Kongzi's method of moral self-cultivation.

The Confucian vision of the ideal society can in some ways be likened to singing in a choir or playing in a symphony orchestra: activities in which one participates to create beauty and harmony beyond the capacity any single individual could achieve on her own.[5] One thing to notice about such analogies is how they highlight the ways in which participating in society affords one *greater* opportunities for expression, meaning, and satisfaction than could be found in any solitary form of life. Almost all modern accounts of society see it as a constraint on personal freedom—the views of Hobbes and Freud are good examples. No doubt society *does* impose limitations upon our activity, and this is equally true of participation in a choir or orchestra, but it is equally true, though often unappreciated, that such activities also broaden and enrich the possibilities of a human life. According to the ideal Confucian model of society, one must develop one's own abilities to participate in such an enterprise and one's "performance" must heed and respond to the efforts of the other members of the "ensemble"; these requirements were regarded, and rightly so, as opportunities to *expand* one's sense of self and to extend and deepen the sources of meaning and satisfaction in one's life. Kongzi cherished music, or at least music of the right sort, because it expressed these ideals of participation, cooperation, and harmony. In *Analects* 3.23 he says, "The proper way to play music may be known. Music begins with playing in unison. When it gets into full swing, it is harmonious, clear, and unbroken; in this way it is carried to its conclusion" (樂其可知也始作翕如也從之純如也皦如也繹如也以成).

Kongzi believed that the right kind of music can have a subtle, almost magical effect upon people, moving them to moral action and inspiring and reshaping their affections and attitudes. In this way music is like the "Virtue" (*de* 德) or "moral charisma" of a morally good ruler or, as seen in texts like the *Mengzi*, like the spontaneous joy and inspiring influence of moral action.[6] We do not have the space to explore in sufficient detail the underlying notions about human physiology and the cosmos that provide much of the support for these beliefs. Briefly and too crudely, they include the belief that human beings share certain innate emotions that can be stimulated and influenced by corresponding arrangements of sounds, not unlike the way a tuning fork will resonate when stimulated by vibrations of a certain frequency. Not only certain sounds, but also more complex phenomena such as dissonance or harmony will elicit characteristic responses from human beings. The important point for our present inquiry is that music is not inert; it acts as a powerful cause in the world, and its effects on human beings can be remarkably subtle, swift, and profound.[7] Music is not just some thing we sit back and listen to or create to express ourselves or entertain others; often it *acts upon* us, helps to shape our feelings and thoughts, and quite literally propels us into action. Music can *move* not only our emotions but also our bodies and minds because there is no clear and definitive separation between these. When music inspires us to more active engagement this often greatly increases the richness of our experience and our overall enjoyment.

The early Chinese believed that music of the right kind both manifests and has the ability to elicit feelings of joy. The two notions—music and joy—were graphically as well as semantically related; as Xunzi noted, citing what was probably a well-known phrase, "Music is joy" (夫樂者樂也).[8] Classical Chinese court music was performed with accompanying pantomime or dance, reinforcing the idea that proper music conveys ideas and attitudes, stimulates the physical body, and sets into motion spontaneous and appropriate behavior. We see these ideas in other passages from the "Record of Music" chapter of the "Book of Rites."

> Now music is joy—what by nature human beings cannot do without. This joy must be expressed in sounds and manifested in movements of the body; such is the way of human beings. . . Singing is a prolonged form of speech. When one is pleased with something, one puts it into words. When putting it into words is not enough, one sings about it. When singing about it is not enough, one sighs and cries over it. When sighing and crying are not enough, before one realizes it, one's hands begin to dance it out and one's feet begin to step in time.

Kongzi claimed that there were two kinds of proper court music. The highest was an expression of complete moral excellence; as such it could stand as the symbol of moral ideals and its motive power could inspire the cultivation of such qualities. Such music was thought to express and elicit specific virtues: unity, orderliness, harmony, and moderation, among others. A good musical composition, like a well-ordered self or state, had a clear unity and order. Within this order, there was harmony among the various instruments and movements of the dance. None was allowed to dominate or stray to excess—hence the piece embodied moderation and discipline. A musical composition that embraced all of these characteristics would "sound" happy, joyful, and well-balanced and would produce corresponding feelings in those who listened to it or observed its performance. An example of this highest form of music was the *Shao*, the court music of the legendary sage emperor Shun. In *Analects* 7.14 we see the profound effect this music had upon Kongzi: "The Master heard the *Shao* in Qi and for three months did not notice the taste of the meat he ate. He said, 'I never dreamt the joys of music could reach such heights!'" (子在齊聞韶三月不知肉味曰不圖為樂之至於斯也). Below the *Shao* was the *Wu*, the court music of the king who overthrew the debauched and wicked last ruler of the Shang dynasty and founded the Zhou dynasty. Kongzi had the following to say about these two kinds of music, "The *Shao* is both perfectly beautiful and perfectly good. The *Wu* is perfectly beautiful but not perfectly good" (*Analects* 3.25) (謂韶盡美矣又盡善也謂武盡美矣未盡善也).[9] The difference, it would seem, is that the former music represented an ideal age of peace and harmony while the later represented an age of righteous conquest. In both, the virtues of unity, order, harmony, and moderation were present but these—particularly the latter two—were more fully expressed in the *Shao* music.

Kongzi believed that music was both an accurate indicator and powerful inculcator of values. Because of the latter belief, he not only advocated the performance and appreciation of certain kinds of music but also argued that bad or harmful music should be banned and eliminated. In *Analects* 15.10 he says, "Banish the songs of Zheng and keep your distance from glib talkers. The songs of Zheng are licentious. Glib talkers are dangerous" (放鄭聲遠佞人鄭聲淫佞人殆). It is important to understand the object and nature of Kongzi's denunciation of the "songs of Zheng" and to make clear that his willingness to ban such music was highly restricted; it did not apply to most forms of music. His call to censor the songs of Zheng expressed his opposition to new forms of *official court music*; he showed no interest at all in criticizing many other new kinds of music that were around in his day. This is clear from passages in the *Analects*, which we will discuss more thoroughly below, that describe Kongzi enjoying and even joining in with others to sing popular music in informal settings and other passages which depict him playing the zither; these passages show no hint of the traditional fidelity that characterizes his views about official court music. A blanket policy of censorship would also foreclose the important diagnostic function of popular music, which Confucians have always valued. Kongzi was a musical traditionalist only when it came to official court music, which was an important part of what we might call official state ceremony. He was strongly opposed to novelty in this realm and sought to ban the music that was being played at some of the courts of his time, but he nowhere showed a lack of appreciation for popular music and this attitude is shared by all early members of the tradition. Mengzi explicitly endorsed the popular music enjoyed by King Hui of Liang and saw value in its ability to bring him to realize that he shares the joy of such music with others (*Mengzi* 1B1). Kongzi was against the subversion of the traditional, ritual music performed by the state. In our own terms, we might think of someone who would oppose changing the national anthem, replacing Hail to the Chief, or performing a hip-hop version of "Taps" at the funeral of a fallen soldier. Kongzi thought official forms of traditional music should not be abandoned, lightly altered, or replaced because they served a variety of ends essential to the preservation of a stable and harmonious society.

Kongzi's distrust of glib talkers was motivated by similar concerns and expresses a view shared by early Daoists as well as Kongzi and his later followers.[10] From the start of their tradition, Confucians have been wary of spoken eloquence, perhaps because they saw, arguably correctly, its immediate, great, and not easily controlled power to persuade and motivate people and feared how easily it could lead them astray. Unlike early Greece and much of the subsequent Western tradition, oratorical eloquence was regarded more with suspicion than admiration in traditional China and this attitude is still quite influential today.[11] Literary masters and accomplished calligraphers and painters were and largely still are more highly prized than eloquent orators, perhaps because while capable of equal power these arts lend themselves to and encourage careful contemplation and assessment.[12] Of course, eloquent and persuasive speech, like the right kind of music, can serve the good or provide a source of deep aesthetic enjoyment as well as lead one astray, and so Confucian teachings about the dangers of "glib talkers" should be understood more as warnings about their potential ill effects at court than as a rejection of oratorical elegance per se.[13]

To help us better understand the subtle, often non-conscious effects of music on human psychology, it might help to consider the similarly subtle ways that we respond to a range of visual stimuli. Many hospitals now shun the "sanitary" white and stainless steel look of years past and decorate their facilities with earth tones and scenes from nature; even doctors and nurses wear green and blue and sport flower motifs on their uniforms. They do this because it has been shown to lower the time their patients spend in hospital, the amount of pain medication they request, and the rate of complaints they make. Dentist offices in many parts of the world include fish tanks, because watching fish swim around lowers patient anxiety. Staring at certain colors, shapes, or scenes affects us in ways most of us do not fully recognize. For example, looking out from a slight rise over an open grassy area bordered by trees and near water, has a deeply soothing, comforting, and empowering effect on us. If you look at the corporate headquarters of most major companies, you will see that their executive offices often afford such a view. This is also why certain real estate is more expensive, why a view of Central Park will cost you dearly if you live in New York City. Many, though not all, of the beliefs of Chinese geomancy, called "Wind and Water" *Fengshui* 風水, can be supported by such facts about human psychology. These inclinations are the hidden legacy of natural selection and evolution; human nature equips, orients, and inclines us in certain ways in regard to music as well.[14]

Since the kind of court music Kongzi advocated usually involved both music and stylized dance, it presented both aural and visual stimulation; the experience would be something like seeing a well-choreographed musical, and this helps to explain the particular attractiveness of this type of production and perhaps its use for political purposes in genres such as Revolutionary Opera.[15] Kongzi's minimal claim—that such performances can inspire emotional and psychological reactions from us—seems eminently defensible and even obvious, which makes our general views about the purely personal nature of music seem implausible and naive. It seems quite likely that such beliefs about music are more a reflection of a particular culture of strong individualism than a plausible account of the nature and function of music. We should be more skeptical about Kongzi's claims regarding a tight and universal correspondence between types of music and types of psychological states, though there is good evidence to support properly modest and qualified forms of many of these claims as well.[16]

Kongzi further insisted that good musical performances manifest and can elicit feelings of unity, order, harmony, and moderation, and this too makes a good deal of sense. We would want to amend such claims to reflect what we know about the cultural specificity of certain aspects of music appreciation; however, such modifications can be made and still accommodate his general point.[17] In particular, the claims that musical performances can manifest and inculcate feelings of group unity, solidarity, and identity are highly plausible and are strengthened when we keep in mind how particular songs can embody and transmit ideas, traditions, and cultures.[18] This is why musical performances and festivals are so widely observed throughout the world. Music has a kind of binding force, drawing together and uniting people. If people will harmonize in song, they will tend to harmonize in purpose and action as well. The unity of the performance has a tendency to spread to and inform other aspects of life. This is why people join together to sing hymns, why there are national anthems, and why people sing songs like "We Shall Overcome" in great movements requiring moral solidarity. In terms of contemporary life, this is why rock concerts have such appeal. They are today's version of religious festivals, though their message often is simply "have fun."[19] Go to a concert and watch what transpires. People will be dressed in the contemporary equivalent of "traditional costumes"—what today we call the latest fashion—they will gather in celebration, dance, and chant the songs of their "sages" and find greater meaning in their lives as they pursue these ends in the shared company of others.[20] These are all profoundly human inclinations; such events should lead us to reflect more carefully and deeply upon what goals they currently serve and what ends they might help us to achieve.

The performance of traditional songs and dances offers another example of the continuity of culture that Kongzi prized so highly. Repeating traditional songs, like performing traditional rituals, maintains continuity across generations and gives people a feeling of being located in a stable, secure, and enduring community. Music not only binds the members of one generation to another; it also can knit successive generations together and weave them into traditions.

All of the features of music that I have mentioned up to now are concerned primarily with the experience of the audience. Kongzi did not discuss the performer's perspective in as much detail but from things he said and what others later said, we can come to understand and appreciate features of this aspect of musical performance as well. We know Kongzi was quite musical himself. He knew how to play the "lute" (se 瑟) (*Analects* 17.20). Whenever he heard someone sing a song he liked, he would wait until the person was done, ask him or her to repeat it, and then join in (*Analects* 7.32). We might speculate a little further. To master an instrument like the *se* requires years of diligent study, usually under the tutelage of a teacher. One studies notes, chords, and scales and progresses to practice the classical works of the tradition. In this process, one moves from rote practice to personal interpretation of and expression through these pieces. As one progresses, one comes to realize the need to inform each performance with one's heart and soul in order to add "life"—or more accurately *humanity*—to the performance. And if one performs in concert with others, one must be highly sensitive to their personal styles and ever aware of one's role in the greater composition. In all these ways, the mastery of a musical instrument resembles the practice of the rites and connects us to different traditions. It is a uniquely human enterprise and a vital expression of our fundamental humanity.

I hope this much too rapid and cursory introduction to early Chinese views of music serves to show how important it was to them—at least the Confucians among them—and how this distinctive cultural practice can and almost inevitably does play an important role in our own moral lives. As I already have argued, a number of these ancient Chinese views about music make eminently good sense. It is highly plausible to take music as a helpful and often remarkably accurate diagnostic of an age. Consider the songs of the 1960s in the United States; they gave voice to the civil rights movement and protests against the Vietnam War, two of the most important themes that defined that decade. The music of this period reveals a great deal about the social and political events of the time and what was going on in the hearts and minds of the people. One would be hard-pressed to find a single, more accurate, precise, or revealing gauge of the age, just as early Confucians maintained. This might and should lead us to ask what the styles and themes of contemporary music tell us about the present age and about ourselves. What does *our* music say? How does it reveal our priorities, express our aspirations, and shape the lives we lead?[21]

When the Rolling Stones toured Mainland China in 2006, the government prohibited them from singing five songs (widely believed to be "Brown Sugar," "Honky Tonk Women," "Beast of Burden," "Let's Spend the Night Together," and "Rough Justice") because of the overly sexual nature of their lyrics and grinding rhythms.[22] Many in the West condemned this government censorship, forgetting or simply not knowing that a similar policy was enforced in the United States early in the rock 'n' roll era. When Elvis Presley first appeared on the *Ed Sullivan Show*, on 9 September 1956, he was shown only from the waist up, when performing, in order to hide the much too suggestive gyrations of "Elvis the pelvis." Despite this precaution, in his review of this event, Jack Gould, of the *New York Times*, criticized the explicitly sexual overtones of Elvis's performance as "a gross national disservice."[23] Elvis's movements were considered sexually suggestive, and some clearly were, but the deeper criticism was that the music itself—the lyrics and most fundamentally the "primitive jungle rhythms"—had an almost irresistible power to seduce the young and elicit licentious feelings, thoughts, and actions.[24]

In contemporary America, many people find certain music unsettling and disturbing; the lyrics of some songs clearly are profoundly violent, hateful, racist, and sexist, and the music is extremely loud, repetitive, and discordant. Why is it wrong to argue against and perhaps even seek to regulate people's exposure to such music? We have several laws regulating pornography and others prohibiting some of its most radical forms; why not legislate against the most disturbing types of music and especially the most blatant forms of violent, hateful, racist, or sexist music? If the ancient Chinese are correct—and there are good reasons to think they are—the baleful influence of the latter can be at least and perhaps even more insidious, potent, and toxic.

It is hard to deny that music both manifests and informs our character, much more than many people recognize or would like to admit. This may not and should not lead one to advocate censorship—as we saw Kongzi did in regard to official court music—but it might well lead one to resist changing certain traditional, social forms of music and speak out against and condemn stupid, vicious, callous, selfish, or shallow music as a menace, a nuisance, a bore, or simply a waste of time. These latter concerns offer solid ground for controlling the dissemination of certain kinds of offensive music: shielding the young and those who do not care to be bombarded by it and the malignant influence it carries. We do this in the case of pornography; a blanket refusal to consider it in the case of music seems to express nothing more than a prejudice against one sense—the visual—over another—the aural. Complete censorship goes much too far, for it discourages the spontaneous exploration and play necessary for the creation of music and that are integral parts of its diagnostic and therapeutic values. Much the same goes for other forms of art as well. Nevertheless, certain restrictions on access and dissemination, similar to what we now practice in regard to pornography, along with an active private-sector tradition of criticism might temper and direct musical activity without frustrating creativity or discouraging play; borrowing a musical metaphor: what we seek is balance and *harmony* among a number of distinct but interrelated goods.

The Confucian tradition teaches us important lessons about the music in and of our lives. Music is not inert; its effects on human beings can be subtle, swift, and profound. It often carries not only ideas but traditions and cultures across time. It is much more powerful and important than we realize. A world without music—like one without ceremony, ritual, or art—would not be a *human* world at all. A world defined by crude, harsh, violent, and uncaring music would be human but utterly *inhumane*.

5

THE VALUES OF FAMILIES

Perhaps the strongest, most widespread and distinctive impression people have of the Confucian tradition is the central role families play in its ethical perspective and in particular the importance of filial piety as a core virtue and characteristic feature of Confucian ethics.[1] Unlike some generalizations, this one is substantially accurate and revealing, though it often relies on a shallow and unflattering caricature of filial piety and can easily lead to the false impression that Confucianism is somehow *anomalous* or even *unique* in seeing families and filial piety as critically important parts of human life. The latter view, the idea that traditions other than Confucianism tend to wholly ignore or have no substantial role for families or filial piety in their descriptions of ethical life, is mistaken and misleading. Families and notions of filial piety have been central concerns for every major culture throughout history, and, as noted in the Introduction, they remain of great and fundamental importance even in the liberal societies within which some ignore, criticize, or dismiss their significance. In this chapter, I would like to explore some of the reasons Confucians give for according such pride of place to families and argue that versions of at least a number of these traditional beliefs remain convincing and even compelling today. Among other things, I will argue that our experiences in the earliest periods of life offer us the first opportunities to develop a sense of ourselves as related to others, our first experiences of being loved for who we are, and our first dim understanding of our mutual interdependence, which can give rise to a sense of having obligations to others and a desire to live in harmony with other human beings and, by extension, the rest of the world.

These early childhood experiences play a critical role in the formation of our basic ethical sensibilities, but families contribute in other profound ways to the development of our moral sensibilities as well.[2] For example, families are where most of us regularly experience both needing and giving aid and care.[3] Kongzi often talks about the care of the elderly as well as the young and this is part of his deep insight into the importance of families—along with close personal relationships—as the source and model for morality. On one occasion, when asked by a disciple to share his personal aspiration, Kongzi replied by saying, "I would like to bring peace to the aged, offer trust to my friends, and cherish the young" (老者安之朋友信之少者懷之) (*Analects* 5.26). Given these and other features of family life, it is quite reasonable to see families as one of the most critical features on the ethical landscape. From the vantage of such a perspective, we can see clear and persuasive reasons for affording families special status within society: an issue at the heart of the so-called public/private debate in contemporary ethical and political theory. As noted earlier, the modern Confucians I envisage would insist that it is wrong to draw a clear, rigid, and impermeable boundary between families and the rest of society, as many modern Western thinkers tend to do. From a Confucian point of view, families serve as the "inner" domestic core around which the "outer" public world takes shape; these two spheres of life are parts of a single continuum across which we regularly cross and within which we live our lives. A distinctive and important feature of the Confucian view of these different aspects of life is that the virtues we need in one sphere, in large measure, are the same as those we need in the other, a point to which we shall return below.

Many modern liberals argue that "the family" is just another social institution, but I shall argue that any robust sense of this claim is simply false. First of all, unqualified, this kind of claim tends to obscure the fact that there are lots of quite different arrangements that all are equally recognized as families; the traditional nuclear family that serves as the widely used conception of "the family" is not and should not be regarded as exhaustive or representative of families in general. Both Kongzi and Menzi were raised in single-parent families, by their mothers. Mengzi's mother is famous throughout East Asia as an exemplary parent and stories about her offer important lessons about early Chinese conceptions of parenting and the lives of women.[4] If we understand the notion of the family as indicating various social groups in which adult members are committed to one another and often take direct care of and responsibility for children, we can address the issues that fall within the range of our concerns in a more comprehensive and revealing manner.

If families indeed are just another kind of social institution, they are defined purely according to social norms, lie wholly within the public realm, and therefore must answer fully to the demands of public ethical concerns, such as social justice. On such a view, as part of the public realm, states determine what does and does not constitute a family, and families should be regulated, policed, and open to legal scrutiny and prosecution, just as any other social institution is, equally under law. While this succeeds in making families answerable to the demands of justice, which often is the primary and most laudable motivation for such arguments, it also provides governments with very powerful warrants to determine definitively what is and is not a family and to intrude into, monitor, and regulate the functioning of families, which worries and disturbs many people.[5]

Modern Confucians embrace the call for greater justice within families, but they reject the idea that families are just another form of social institution and they are right to do so. Like some in the West who seek to defend certain conceptions of the family, traditional Confucians have appealed to a Heavenly-based natural order to support the special status of families. I am not concerned with endorsing, refuting, or even fully engaging such arguments here.[6]

Instead, I suggest that there are a number of very good arguments that rely only upon general features of human nature and moral psychology for according families special status as uniquely important social institutions. Such an approach accepts the irrefutable fact that the natural needs and capacities that underlie the formation of families can find a variety of equally acceptable forms or expressions. In other words, the view I defend is not committed to there being any single or definitive form a family must take.

Most versions of the claim that families are just another social institution are deeply at odds with what we know about human evolution. Unlike modern states and their institutions, family groupings are not purely or even primarily artifacts of human ingenuity; they are based upon millions of years of evolution. Contrary to the myth that some philosophers use to make plausible the idea that society is a kind of contract that independent, mature, and free-roving human beings designed and entered into at some point in history, human beings and their biological ancestors never lived such independent and autonomous lives.[7] We have always been social animals, and within human societies, we always have organized ourselves into family units.[8] The latter have been, as Confucians claim, the basis upon which the former took shape. This is not an expression or endorsement of the idea that biology is destiny, if we mean by such a claim that biology *determines* every significant feature of our lives, relationships, and communities; as noted earlier, the needs and capacities with which we are endowed leave us considerable latitude about how we structure and regard families within a particular society. What modern Confucians do reject, as everyone should, is the idea that biology plays no significant role in the kinds of organizations that human beings in fact tend to choose and value. At the extreme, such a view dissolves into nonsense, for it deprives us of any meaningful basis for understanding or justifying the preferences we have or the choices we make.

Throughout the long course of human evolution, families have been necessary for successfully bearing and nurturing children as well as protecting and caring for the aged; these activities placed considerable constraints on what kinds of groups and relationships constituted successful families. To insist that the deep and complex imprint these evolutionary forces have left upon us can be effaced or eliminated by embracing some new conception of what human life should be is naive, rash, and of dubious value, for reasons that I shall make clear below. Most important for the arguments I shall advance is the fact that human families, whatever their structure or form, must provide children with sustained and highly focused love and attention for extended periods of time. This in turn requires that adult members of such families must be committed not only to each other but also to their families.[9] They must be willing to dedicate great amounts of time, resources, and energy to maintaining and nurturing their families and must subordinate most other kinds of personal enjoyment and gratification for the particular sense of accomplishment and satisfaction that is found in being a member of a well-functioning family. In sum, it is not plausible to maintain that families are social constructs that are, like the Internal Revenue Service, cut from whole cloth under the guidance and through the power of human ingenuity in order to meet contingent social needs or desires. Things work very much in the opposite direction. Rather than being pure artifacts, families arise out of and reflect fundamental features of human nature. They are more like the domestic varieties of rice or wheat that we eat today, which have been developed out of earlier, naturally occurring wild varieties, than examples of technological innovation such as cell phones, whose form and function first took shape in human imagination.

The next issue I would like to explore concerns the distinctive and still influential view in Western political philosophy and culture that sees the private and the public as two distinct and separate "realms" or "worlds"; as noted earlier, this has given rise to what is widely known as the public-private debate. The public-private debate contains a rich and diverse set of views and arguments. The particular form of the distinction that I have in mind is historically important and remains highly influential; it presents public and private as two distinct realms of life and describes them as different worlds or environments with different corresponding modes of living.[10] Traditionally, the private realm is a world of shared love, support, generosity, and warmth where virtues like justice are not needed and appear to have no significant role to play. It finds its clearest exemplar in the harmonious interactions among the members of an ideal family. In contrast, the public realm is a world of mutual aggression, competition, greed, and hostility—it's a jungle out there—where principles like fairness and virtues like justice must work mightily in order to prevent a general collapse into an unregulated war of all against all. It is apparent that this picture of the public and private realms is not only a description of different purported aspects of human life; it also strongly implies different normative standards for each of these two contrasting ethical worlds. The virtues appropriate for the warm and loving private or domestic realm cannot survive or function in the harsh and competitive public world, and the stern and strong virtues of the public realm have no place and are not welcome within families. We are to abandon the fierce and warlike virtues we employ in the public realm at the threshold of our homes as we enter the warm embrace of our families. We must leave behind the love and trust that define domestic life each morning when we part from our families and enter once more into the breach to do battle in the uncaring public realm. This kind of view has been used to argue for an unequal "natural" division of labor between women and men, with women regarded as better "equipped" and inclined for success in the domestic realm and men naturally "suited" for work in the public realm. This, of course, tends strongly and unjustly to restrict women to the private sphere of "the family" and deny them access to the range of challenges and satisfactions that can only be found in the public realm. Much excellent work has been done exposing the flaws in such traditional conceptions and seeking to overturn the patriarchal implications of the public-private distinction, but that is an issue I will not be delving into here.[11] Instead of considering the legitimacy of a gendered division of labor based upon a particular conception of public and private, I want to explore the more fundamental question of the legitimacy of this widely held view about public and private realms. As we shall see, even the most traditional

Confucians reject the kind of strict division between public and private that I have been describing and that serves as the basis for a gender-based division of labor; modern Confucians maintain this traditional point of view as well and argue that the very effort to sever the link between the private and public aspects of human life and view them as wholly different and unconnected ethical worlds is deeply misguided.

The Confucian perspective offers a distinctive and in many respects better way to think about the relationship between families and public life. The closest parallels in traditional Chinese thought to the paired concepts private and public are the terms "inside" (*nei* 內) and "outside" (*wai* 外). Each of these terms has a range of meanings, but for our purposes we will focus upon their senses in the context of families and their place in the larger social order. In many contexts, *nei* refers to actions and events in the "inner" sphere of the family as opposed to the "outer" public arenas of life, but, unlike private and public, *nei* and *wai* are not regarded as unconnected and wholly distinct spheres or worlds. Indeed to imply that one's inner and outer lives are anything less than intimately connected and mutually influential, much less wholly separate, would indicate a profound malady. In the case of the self, it would constitute a form of schizophrenia.[12] The implication is much the same in the case of the relationship between families and the rest of society. The contemporary scholar of Chinese and comparative feminisms, Pauline Chen Lee has described many of the distinctive features of *nei* and *wai* and compared them with the corresponding Western notions of private and public in highly revealing ways.[13] Among the many helpful points she makes is that in contrast to any strict and clear separation, *nei* and *wai* share a flexible and permeable boundary; the line between them is like the border between different states within the same country: it marks different parts of a shared territory, often follows no straight or geometric pattern, and is a border that is regularly crossed as people engage in the business of life. For our purposes, this is one of the most important features of the Confucian view: ethically speaking, *nei* and *wai* are not discontinuous or fundamentally distinct; they not only are connected but also are similar in nature, different aspects of a single, unified whole. A critical implication of this view is that the virtues needed "inside," in the more intimate parts of one's life, are for the most part the same as those needed "outside," in the shared, public realm.[14]

Traditional Confucian conceptions of filial piety do insist on certain special duties to parents. The degree of deference, attention, and care one is to devote to one's parents distinguishes the *degree* to which one is to express certain virtues in the private versus the public realms. Nevertheless, one is to be filial, benevolent, courageous, conscientious, and so forth, outside as well as within the family.[15] In fact, in Confucian writings, a good family often is used as a *paradigm* for the state; the ideal ruler is to think of and work for his subjects in much the same way a loving parent is dedicated to the welfare of her or his children. The Confucian ideal is to extend the virtues one first cultivates in the family to the rest of society and the world until one regards all other people as more distant kin. Kongzi's moving and inspirational ideal community is not a *polis* led by elite politician-warriors, nor a Kingdom of Ends, but roughly the family writ large, a society in which, as noted earlier, as it says in *Analects* 12.5, "all within the four seas are brothers." This idea remains an important feature of contemporary Chinese culture within which people call and refer to one another using familial terms such as "sister" (*jiejie* 姐姐), "brother" (*didi* 弟弟), "aunt" (*ayi* 阿姨), and "uncle" (*shushu* 叔叔). We are to be loyal, courageous, loving, generous, trustworthy and so forth, at home, in our home society, and abroad in the wide world—though to varying degrees and according to context.

In Confucianism, there is no strong division into separate realms of activity, no contrast between a caring and nurturing inner life and a harsh and competitive outer life. What in the West are seen as separate spheres is regarded as a unified and continuous whole. This is not to say that the inner and outer aspects of our lives are identical; there is always greater intimacy within the family than there is out in the public realm. This, though, does not mean one can never find deep and intimate relationships out in the public realm. In fact, we do find such relationships and in various forms. We normally meet our future spouses in the course of living our *public* lives and this is where we form deep and lasting friendships as well. In the former case, one's relationship transforms a fellow worker or acquaintance into a member of one's family; in the latter, we often come to regard our closest friends as "one of the family," a change we often mark by having our children refer to them as "aunt" or "uncle." In other words, when we develop such special relationships these people pass from the "outer" realm into our "inner," more intimate, circle of life. These features of everyday human experience only serve to support the Chinese perspective of inner and outer as constituents of a unified and continuous whole, two different aspects of life separated by an indefinite, flexible, and permeable boundary.

Another difference between the inner and outer aspects of life is that the former is the source of and, as noted earlier, often the model for many of the ethical sensibilities and principles that govern and inform behavior in the latter. This brings us not only to an important feature of the relationship between the inner and outer realms but also to one of the most important reasons modern Confucians and all the rest of us as well have for rejecting the ethical bifurcation of human life into public and private and for insisting on the special status of families. Like much of contemporary ethical and political philosophy, the reigning views about the public and private realms do not offer a careful and plausible moral psychology and are especially inadequate when it comes to providing an account of how we develop the sensibilities, attitudes, and commitments needed to live as decent members of society.[16] Modern Confucians argue that this failure is for the most part the result of not appreciating the ways in which our various moral sensibilities arise and mature within the context of our families. In other words, from the Confucian point of view, ethicists and political theorists must come to understand and fully appreciate the unique role that loving families play in the growth and maintenance of moral sensibility and understanding.[17]

Confucians claim families are both the source and paradigm of virtue. Roughly, what they mean by the former is that we first experience and develop our sense of what it is to care for another for the sake of the other within the context of our families. The care and attention primary caregivers—usually but not necessarily biological parents—provide for very young children is the child's first experience of this fundamental other-regarding attitude. The spontaneous feeling of being indebted and obligated to respond in kind to such treatment marks the first stirrings of a range of other ethical attitudes as well; one could describe this as the birth of our moral conscience. Confucians believe, and there is considerable plausibility in their claim, that as a matter of practical human psychology, an ethical stance on the world is founded on the experiences of love, care, sacrifice, and generosity that mark good families. Not only core virtues but also our sense of ourselves as autonomous moral agents first arise in the context of familial love and, as noted earlier, in activities like play,[18] and not, as many contemporary Western ethicists claim, in the course of exercising sophisticated rational abilities.[19] Contrary to a good deal of contemporary philosophy and widespread popular opinion, love and care are not blind feelings or unruly emotions; they involve the orientation and development of our intentions and commitments. The famous and highly influential neo-Confucian thinker Zhu Xi 朱熹 (1130–1200) once explained that an "intention" or "commitment" (*zhi* 志) is "that which the heart and mind pursues" (心之所之).[20] The focus or orientation of the heart and mind defines what and who we are and plays a direct and commanding role in our identities as ethical beings. Confucians further argue that good families often serve as the conceptual paradigm for how good rulers should regard and act toward those for whom they are responsible. Traditionally, such beliefs arose in a context in which absolute monarchy was the assumed form of government, but if we generalize and take the main point of this latter claim to be that rulers should show the kind of concern for their citizens—a number of whom of course *are* children or aged—that good parents show for their children and elders, there is much to admire in such a view.[21]

We can easily extend this insight about how we often come to understand and act ethically in the outer, public realm by modeling familiar familial relationships. When we attempt to persuade others to develop greater ethical concern for people they do not know, it is not uncommon for us to draw analogies between the hypo- thetical treatment of family members and the anonymous others we hope will enjoy greater understanding and care. Many people may begin by expressing relative indifference to how strangers are treated, but if we ask them to imagine how they would feel if their mother, father, sister, brother, or children were the objects of such indifference, often they will begin to recognize and feel the force of such appeals. This is because they *already* bring to such imaginary scenarios a strong commitment and active concern for the well- being of family members. And so, it is often by "extending" natural familial feelings that we develop and successfully act as moral mem- bers of society. This idea is presented in a famous passage from the *Mengzi* in which Mengzi seeks to move King Xuan of Qi to feel appropriate concern for his people by explaining how King Wen was able to apply his caring heart to all within the four seas.

> And so those who are able to extend their kindness will
>   be able to care for all within the four seas; those who
>   cannot extend their kindness will be unable to care for
>   their own wife and children. The respect in which the
>   ancients greatly surpassed the average human being was
>   nothing other than the extent to which they excelled at
>   extending what they did. Now your kindness is sufficient
>   to reach to animals and yet you make no effort to care
>   for your people. Why is this case special? (*Mengzi* 1A7)[22]

An excellent illustration of how natural familial feelings serve as the source of more general ethical virtues is the well-known story *Pinocchio*, in which the little wooden puppet of the same name aspires to become *a real boy* by proving himself brave, truthful, and most importantly *unselfish*. While quickly learning what and how admirable these qualities are and that they are the means to realizing his greatest desire, Pinocchio repeatedly fails to develop or display these virtues. It is only when he discovers that his adoptive father, Geppetto, has been swallowed by a whale while venturing out to sea in an effort to rescue Pinocchio from the grim fate that awaited him on Pleasure Island—a hedonic paradise where young boys are led by their uncontrolled desires literally to make jackasses out of themselves—that Pinocchio immediately embodies all three virtues. His willingness to risk and even sacrifice his own life in order to save his father demonstrates his virtue, and he is rewarded by being transformed through the magical intervention of the patient and loving Blue Fairy into a real boy, realizing the wish he made upon a star at the beginning of the story. From the start, Pinocchio cognitively understands what the virtues are and that they define what it is to be good. He has the added motivation of knowing that developing these traits of character is the one sure way to realizing his greatest wish: to become a real boy. In addition, he has the great advantage of receiving regular and reliable moral advice from Jiminy Cricket, who serves as Pinocchio's "conscience" throughout the course of his adventures. And yet, it is only his strong and unwavering love for his father that inspires, guides, and sustains him to develop the virtues and thereby transform himself from a puppet into a human being.

All of the arguments presented above, especially the one about families being the source of many of our most basic moral sensibilities, offer strong reasons for rejecting the modern view of families as simply one more social institution and instead recognizing families as the unique and critical phenomenon they surely are. Not only are families distinctive for being founded on special, intimate relationships, but those relationships are the bases for many, perhaps most, of our moral sensibilities. Families are where our moral sensibilities first germinate and these sensibilities begin as highly particular relationships of care, love, and devotion. Unless they take root in the nourishing soil of good family life, these fundamental moral attitudes cannot or at least are much less likely to germinate, grow, and mature into full virtue. Important virtues like justice, in the sense of disinterested fairness, play almost no role in the early stages of our moral lives and conflict with those emotions and attitudes that constitute and sustain families.[23] Infants and very young children do not need and cannot be helped by disinterested treatment; they need person-specific, highly focused, unqualified love and attention. This is not to say that justice does not play an important role between more mature members of families; of course it does. Even here, though, our attention to the demands of justice is guided and grounded, at least initially, by love for and commitment to the members of a group of intimates. We come to appreciate the value of justice in the context of a group of people we *already* care for deeply, against a background of established trust, and in the course of spontaneous play; we then learn to extend this principle to those we do not know, at first, often through participating in games of various sorts. Natural bonds of affection provide the ground and set the stage for the development of more complex moral sensibilities in the same way they provided the ground and stage for the development of human language and reasoning in general.[24] While justice should govern important aspects of our relationships with those we love and needs theoretical reflection in order to develop fully, it does not dominate or set the standard within families as it does in our public life, and it should not. In fact, within the family, justice most often serves as a guide or fallback position, something we need and appeal to when virtues like care fail to achieve their proper aim.[25] Justice tends to require an impersonal perspective and approach that is inimical to the deep and intense bonds that hold families together and allow them to serve as the incubators of moral sensibilities. For all these reasons, Confucians reject the claim that families are just another sort of social institution and instead see families as first and foremost among such institutions.

6

AWARENESS, ATTENTIVENESS, AND CARE IN AND OF THE EVERYDAY

In this chapter, I shall argue that Kongzi's Way offers an interesting combination of utopian aspiration and quotidian concern and that one of its most distinctive characteristics and greatest contributions is its advocacy of the latter and its insistence that the only way we can work toward our grander social and political goals is by attending to and building out from the everyday. While these features of the Confucian tradition, historically, have resulted in some imprecision and vagueness in regard to political policies and theories, issues which I will explore in more detail below, they also bring a number of distinctive and important strengths.[1] Most importantly, Kongzi's view avoids some of the worst flaws of overly optimistic hopes for the future by focusing our attention on the need first to improve ourselves and only then to work on improving the lives of those around us, the greater society in which we live, and the world we all share. Starting with the self and extending one's concern until it touches even the most distant parts of the world keeps the Confucian pursuit of the Way focused on the importance of the everyday and serves as a brake on the excesses that normally accompany utopian projects. The social and political aspects of Kongzi's *Dao* are more a vision than a plan, expressing our hope for the future, inspired by the past, through our commitment to the present.

Kongzi's way of combining ideal aspiration and quotidian concern distinguishes his theory and approach from most other forms of utopianism by heading off any attempt to directly and immediately bring about the ideal by sacrificing the actual lives people presently are leading, those distant from as well as those close to us. Such desire for direct and immediate realization of the ideal is endemic to many forms of utopianism and the underlying cause is easy to understand. If it seems even merely *possible* to bring about a *perfect* society or move "history" forward toward such an end, great sacrifices not only seem permissible but present themselves as imperatives.[2] This way of thinking is used to justify a great deal of everyday self-centeredness, many bad national policies, and numerous bloody revolutions; it shows how utopianism often opens the door to and pushes even well-intentioned people across the threshold and into the realms of inattentiveness, indifference, and at times great wickedness.[3]

Kongzi's Way does not instigate and works to avoid such a tendency and this close relationship between a gradual development of the self, based in everyday life, and the realization of larger social and political ends is seen in numerous other arguments early Confucians make. For example, Mengzi argues that the *only* way to a stable, wealthy, and powerful society is to ensure that one's ruler and society are ethically good. Some have mistaken him to be making a sly argument based on enlightened self-interest: *if* you, as ruler, want to have a stable, wealthy, and powerful state you must first make yourself into an ethical ruler. In other words: *be* good and you can get everything you want! The difficulties with such a position are clear and have been explored in greater detail in chapter two of this volume: roughly put, in order to succeed in *becoming* ethical, one has to take being good as one's *primary* concern, but this is just what such rulers cannot or will not do.[4] They regard "being good" simply as an effective means to realize self-centered aims. If they somehow *were* sincerely able to take up the perspective they need to become good, their original, self-centered desires and way of life would lose their grip upon them. They would no longer be employing a clever plan in which ethical means are used to attain self-centered ends; they would be transformed and become committed to the good; they would act out of virtuous dispositions. Rulers who managed to do this would be like the sage-king Shun, who "acted out of benevolence and right; he did not simply act benevolently and rightly" (由仁義行非行仁義也) (*Mengzi* 4B19).

The difficulties I have discussed above disappear if we take Mengzi simply to be *describing* the relationship between morality and a stable, wealthy, and powerful state. We should understand him to be declaring to the rulers of his time that *only* states ruled by ethically good people are able to prosper fully and maintain such success over the long run. Further evidence that this is how we should understand him can be found in his additional argument that *only* ethically good rulers *really* are happy. This seems hopelessly naive, if we take him to be saying that bad people are never happy, but it makes perfect sense if we take him to be saying that only good rulers can take joy over many years in the way they attain stability, wealth, and power. In other words, such rulers have the chance to enjoy distinctive and particularly profound senses of satisfaction and joy, but in order to work toward these they must fully and sincerely commit themselves to the Way. The argument is similar to the idea that only those who play fairly can enjoy a proper sense of accomplishment; their victories offer *more than* can be had by those who win by cheating or treachery; fair players take satisfaction in what they are and how they played, even in cases when they do not win. The important point for our current concern is that one cannot work toward or realize grand social or political ideals by discounting or ignoring people's everyday lives. One can only approach the ideal by building upon and enhancing the actual and everyday, beginning always with one's self.

Kongzi clearly aimed to move society toward a utopian ideal, one which he understood as having been practiced in earlier times, most clearly in the Golden Age of the Zhou dynasty. In previous chapters, we noted *Analects* 12.5, which expresses this ideal in terms of the family writ large; we are to see a world in which "all within the four seas are brothers." Later Confucians described this ideal in other ways as well. For example, in the "Evolution of the Rites"(*Liyun* 禮運) chapter of the *Book of Rites* we are told of an ideal age in which "the world is for everyone" (*tianxia wei gong* 天下爲公); in the same work, this is called the period of "Great Unity" (*Datong* 大同). Apart from such general descriptions about the ethical spirit that characterizes such a society, we are not given many details about or theoretical justifications for its structure, design, or function. In a certain sense, this is to be expected since the ideal society is modeled on the family and led by a good king, who plays the role of parent to his people; such a state is governed by the kind of love, generosity, and devotion that characterizes families. This gives rise to the imprecision and vagueness mentioned in the opening lines of this chapter; the Confucian tradition tends to focus on the general features and animating *spirit* of the ideal society but leaves most of its details and theoretical underpinnings unspecified.[5] While later Confucians do offer careful descriptions of the institutions that supported imperial rule we don't find many detailed theoretical discussions about how these political institutions and procedures establish, maintain, and justify the good society, just as there are few discussions about the institutions and procedures needed to support families. If we assume universal benevolence and generosity, we put our faith, attention, and energy on the spirit and leave the particulars of social and political organization to be worked out by the good people who run them. Given the aforementioned premise that the only way to move toward the ideal society is by improving the self and the lives of those around one, this theoretical weakness came with a complementary and eminently important, more practically oriented strength: it produced remarkable analyses of how one was to develop oneself and educate others in order to move toward the ideal. The value of this approach remains even in the context of very different political systems. For example, it has much to recommend to liberal democracies and can augment some of the best strains within them.[6]

As a critical part of this general concern with self-improvement, Confucians throughout the ages have cultivated an acute sense of awareness about, attention toward, and care for the everyday: concentrating on our interactions with others, intimate as well as distant, and grounded in a regimen of internal monitoring and self-scrutiny.[7] Their belief has always been that focusing upon the quotidian aspects of our behaviors and inner lives plays a crucial role in the development of ourselves. As part of this perspective, they held that we are responsible for and can control and shape not only what we do and say, but what we think and feel, how we comport ourselves in the world, and what we choose to focus on each day. This offers a fairly dramatic contrast with the general attitude of contemporary Western ethics, which tends to hold people responsible for what they do but maintains that we cannot control and therefore are not responsible for what we believe or feel.[8] Confucians insist that we must "carefully watch over" ourselves, not just to restrain the bad tendencies we might have, but equally to notice, develop, and take joy in our better inclinations. They insist that we have the capacity to control and guide our attention and that we must work to focus it upon the most inspiring things we can: our most admirable thoughts, feelings, and aspirations, the most edifying examples and ideals available, as well as the best features of the world.[9]

This represents a characteristically Confucian perspective on human moral freedom. Roughly speaking, freedom lies in the power to turn our attention away from bad inclinations and influences and focus upon the better parts, what Lincoln called "the better angels of our nature,"[10] and the most admirable aspects of culture and the world; moral success and failure, along with praise and blame, are conceived of and assessed in terms of how well we perform this task over time. The Confucian view offers a clear alternative to the modern Western conception of "free will," which tends to employ and rely upon a separate executive power that purportedly can directly control behavior and that focuses upon individual moments of choice. We could characterize this difference by saying that for Confucians, the freedom of human agency is more a matter of steering then rowing. Their goal is to cultivate a greater awareness, attentiveness, and care for our thoughts and feelings, our actions, speech, comportment, and demeanor, the clothes we wear, the music we play and listen to, and how we conduct ourselves in our interactions with fellow human beings, other creatures, and the greater natural world. When we fail to do what we know we should do or do what we know we should not, the failure is not described as owing to a lack of *willpower* but rather to an lack of proper ideals and models or sustained reflection and concentration. If we do not stay focused on the right kinds of things, over time, this produces inattentiveness, insensitivity, poor perception, bad dispositions, and inappropriate behavior.

Such an attitude can and is intended to transform a mundane and uninspired view of everyday life into a challenging and fulfilling task, a form of "spiritual practice" (*gongfu* 功夫).[11] Instead of just passing or marking time we are to focus our lives upon the Way—as Kongzi did when he "committed himself to learning" at the age of fifteen, and this requires us to attend to and cultivate a heightened awareness of ourselves and our surroundings.[12] Such ideas were taken to new levels of sophistication in the philosophy of later Confucians such as Wang Yangming 王陽明 (1492–1529 CE), who urged that "one must, at all times, be like a cat catching mice—with eyes intently watching and ears intently listening" (常如貓之捕鼠一眼看著一耳聽著).[13] The thought is that we are to approach the various tasks we undertake each day not just as things to be done but opportunities to train and develop ourselves. Such concern should not be pursued as a frenetic obsession with one's own moral improvement; this would be to miss the point and distort the purpose of the awareness and attentiveness Confucians recommend. Paying attention to and caring for the everyday is not just or even primarily concerned with the self but with the lives of those around one and ultimately with the general welfare of the world; it aims at cultivating a greater sense of appreciation for the various goods life has to offer as well as at improvement of the self. One of the clearest results of such a life is a deeper understanding of and joy in the course of daily routine. This kind of spiritual practice has the ability to reveal something remarkable in the oft-neglected corners of the everyday, and this is what I shall seek to describe and illustrate in the remaining sections of this chapter.

Many of the most distinctive and important contributions the Confucian tradition makes to our understanding of the human good arise from its characteristic concern with the cultivation of the self and in particular with its advocacy of greater awareness and reflection as foundations for and central constituents of such effort. Such concerns constitute a kind of engaged, more kinetic form of meditative practice that we in the contemporary world would do well to embrace. What I have in mind is only distantly related to more familiar Daoist and Buddhist forms of meditation or the formal regimen known as "quiet sitting" (*jingzuo* 静坐) followed by later Confucians.[14] It is more closely akin to the practices of early Confucians who do not seem to have followed anything as precise and formal as the Daoist, Buddhist, or neo-Confucian regimens mentioned above. Nevertheless, as the following quotation and related references show, their practices did include regular attention to and reflection upon set themes and particular concerns.[15]

> Zengzi said, "Each day I reflect upon three aspects of myself. In my dealings with others, have I been conscientious? In my exchanges with friends and acquaintances have I been true? Have I failed to practice what I have been taught?" (*Analects* 1.4; Cf. 5.27)

One can see related concerns among early Confucians with the effects of and cultivation of different kinds of "energies" (*qi* 氣) and the relationships these have with various moral psychological states. For example, in the *Mengzi* we find passages that make explicit connections between moral psychological states and specific kinds of *qi*, such as the atmospheric *qi* we encounter in the calm hours of dawn, just as the sun rises, which he refers to as the "early morning *qi*" (平坦之氣) (*Mengzi* 6A8), or the special fount of moral motivation and courage that Mengzi calls the "flood-like *qi*" (浩然之氣) (*Mengzi* 2A2). The kinds of reflective practice seen in these passages are comparable to the kinds of training one must undergo to develop other types of desirable abilities or sensibilities, and in fact Confucians often draw explicit analogies between learning the Way and acquiring valuable skills and arts. As we saw in chapter three, Confucians liken moral cultivation to archery. This demanding martial discipline offers a particularly clear and powerful comparative model and is especially effective in conveying the degree to which improving the self requires heightened awareness and attentiveness as well as sustained critical reflection and evaluation.[16]

> Benevolence is like archery. An archer assumes the proper stance and only then releases his arrow. If he fails to hit the mark he does not resent those who best him but turns to find the cause within himself. (*Mengzi* 2A7)

Those who "aim" at improving themselves as opposed to hitting an archery target also need to pay attention to their stance and monitor their inner states, and such concerns led Confucians to advocate what appears to many modern people as an excessive attention to the minutia of everyday action, speech, comportment, and demeanor. As we noted in earlier chapters, such attention extends to the clothes we wear and the music we listen to; such everyday features of the world were thought to both express how we think and feel and shape our character. Surely Confucians are right to insist that these things do play a role both in what we think and feel and in our example to and influence upon others. Sitting or standing up straight instead of slouching both makes one more attentive and alert and expresses greater interest and engagement; wearing clean and well-kept clothes puts one in the right frame of mind and expresses pride in ourselves. We see this kind of attention to everyday practices in Stevie Wonder's classic song "Living for the City," when he describes the noble sister as someone who has to get up early in order to get to school on time and whose clothes are old but never dirty. Like many passages from the *Analects*, these lyrics capture an entire attitude toward a form of life in a short couplet.[17]

Those who adopt the Confucian point of view about the importance of the everyday will carefully watch over themselves. They will keep in their hearts and minds Kongzi's teachings that "clever words and an insinuating appearance rarely express benevolence" (巧言令色鮮矣仁) (*Analects* 17.17), and "cultivated people are modest in what they claim and excel in what they do" (君子恥其

言而過其行) (*Analects* 14.29). They will also be more reflective and fastidious about how they make use of things in the world. They will seek to manifest the care they take with their inner life in their interactions with the artifacts of our culturally constructed world as well. Kongzi exercised great care in how he comported himself toward the things that constitute our social world: "If his mat was not straight, he would not sit upon it" (席不正不坐) (*Analects* 10.9), and he regulated his behavior in light of his surroundings and context: "When he entered the Ancestral Temple, he asked about everything" (入太廟每事問) (*Analects* 10.14). Such concerns may strike many today as insignificant, excessive, or even obsessive, but I don't see why we must or should regard them in these ways. For example, we might adapt Kongzi's practice of asking about everything in the ancestral temple and make it *our* practice to inquire about the cultural treasures of other people when we visit their countries, the religious symbols and rituals of those we meet when we encounter them in the course of our lives, and the possessions people put on display when we enter their homes as guests. Not only will such practices help us to understand more about these people and the lives they live, the very act of asking about such things will help develop as well as express and convey our respect for and interest in them.[18] Of course we have to *sincerely* be interested in them, and this fills out the picture we have been drawing of awareness and attentiveness both to the world around one and to one's own inner states. This shows the importance of and connection between the inner and outer aspects of cultivation and makes clear that the general aim and result of such engaged, kinetic meditation is to help produce more humane ways of interacting with the people, creatures, and things of the world. As one of Kongzi's disciples made clear, "In practicing the rituals the most important thing is a feeling of harmony. This is what made the Way of the former kings so fine; in matters great and small they acted in this manner" (禮之用和為貴先王之道斯為美小大由之) (*Analects* 1.12).

Ultimately, Confucians seek to regard every aspect of the world around them as significant and meaningful: to be more aware, attentive, attuned, and caring about themselves and their interaction with the world; for them *the secular is sacred*. We are told that "the Master fished but would not use a net; shot but never at a resting bird" (子釣而不綱弋不射宿) (*Analects* 7.26). One might simply dismiss such passages as throw-away lines about a quaint, distant, and idealized world, but this would be to ignore the fact that many anglers and hunters today take such matters very seriously, and they are right to do so. Whether one angles with a barbed or barbless hook, light or heavy line and tackle, whether one hunts with bow or rifle, uses or refuses to use bait, takes or foregoes taking a long shot, and so forth, marks one not just as a certain kind of *angler* or *hunter* but also as a certain kind of *person*. These are ways to both cultivate and express respect, care, and reverence for the world. Kongzi extended this kind of awareness, attentiveness, and care to many aspects of the greater natural world and this led him to see many important lessons in Nature. For Kongzi, Nature could serve as revelation and offer genuine epiphanies; once, when standing above a flowing stream, he was inspired to exclaim, "It passes on like this, does it not?—never ceasing day or night!" (逝者如斯夫不舍晝夜) (*Analects* 9.16).[19] The unceasing flow of the stream illustrated to him the power of acting out of one's nature as well as the need to persevere and make constant effort.

As noted in the opening sections of this chapter, Kongzi's Way offers both a personal as well as a social and political ideal. Like all ethical views, it calls on us to be more than what we are, but it does not demand that we sacrifice the more familiar goods of everyday human existence in order to realize its more exalted aims. To the contrary, as I have argued above, it insists that the only way we can possibly realize its grand social and political aims is by developing ourselves, improving our families, and enhancing the lives and institutions around us. This progression from the inner self to the outer world is represented in numerous Confucian texts but perhaps most clearly and memorably in the opening chapter of the *Great Learning* (*Daxue* 大學).

> When things are investigated, knowledge is extended.
> When knowledge is extended, thoughts are sincere.

> When thoughts are sincere, the heart and mind is correct.
> When the heart and mind is correct, the self is cultivated.
> When the self is cultivated, families are properly regulated.
> When families are properly regulated, states are well
>   ordered.
> When states are well ordered, the entire world is at peace.

The Confucian Way presents a lofty spiritual goal but never loses sight of the idea that we begin and move toward this ideal by working to make ourselves better. While Confucians are clear that "the burden is heavy and the Way long" (任重而道遠) (*Analects* 8.7), they are also clear that for them being *on the Way* is where we start and how we make progress; at the end of the day, this is all we can ask of ourselves or one another. Whether or not we succeed in realizing the more utopian goals of the tradition is something ultimately beyond human control; what is within our control is to make a sincere and determined effort. Such effort defines the most critical and characteristic feature of a good life.

In one particularly poignant passage, someone describes Kongzi as "one who knows it won't work out but keeps at it" (知其不可而為之者) (*Analects* 14.41). I believe he would have embraced this chiding description of himself and his work and taken it as an accurate and important testament of his devotion to the Way. This phrase would make a fitting epitaph for Kongzi or any good person; it is an expression of realism, not resignation or disappointment. The best ideals or principles have no real chance of being perfectly realized and sustained in the actual world. As John Rawls saw clearly, we will never live in a perfectly just society: random factors such as the natural lottery are enough to guarantee that will never come to pass. Put in more Confucian terms, I may well never be as good a son, brother, husband, father, or friend as I should be. These admissions, though, do nothing to diminish the value and appeal of perfect justice or being an ideal son, brother, husband, father, or friend. If we live well, we live in light of, aiming at, and striving toward these unrealizable ideals. We "know it won't work out but keep at it," because that is what decent people do.[20] We encourage and support one another, at times leading, at times following, at times leaning upon one another, as we move forward along the Way.

In this chapter, I have argued and sought to illustrate that while Kongzi's Way aims at lofty social and political ideals, it insists that we can pursue such aims only through the everyday. The Way requires us to cultivate much greater awareness, attentiveness, and care for what goes on in the more mundane events of our daily lives; this is not only a critical feature of the Confucian tradition but one that recommends itself to contemporary people of every culture and persuasion. As a final example of this feature of Confucianism, I would like to present and briefly comment upon one of my favorite passages from the *Analects*.

In *Analects* 11.26, Kongzi asks various disciples to tell him what they would like to accomplish should some ruler recognize their talents and potential, offer them employment, and provide the opportunity to pursue their highest aspirations. Zilu answers first and quickly, describing how he would like to take a large state besieged by its neighbors and suffering from famine and, within three years' time, teach its people to be courageous and disciplined. The disciple Qiu answers next saying how he would like to take a moderately sized state and within three years' time lead its people to enjoy material abundance. More modestly, he says he would then await the coming of a true gentleman who could teach the people about ritual and music. Chi follows, saying that he hopes to learn how to serve as an assistant dealing with affairs of state or serving in the Ancestral Temple. Last of all, Kongzi asks Dian for his aspiration. Setting aside the lute he was playing, he rises and while the strings of his instrument are still vibrating Dian declares that his aspiration is different from those of the others. With Kongzi's encouragement he describes what he would like to do.

> In the waning days of spring, wearing the new clothes of
>   the season, with five or six young men and six or seven
>   boys, to bathe in the River Yi, dry ourselves in the gentle
>   breezes to be found at the Altar of Rain and then,
>   together, to return home chanting.

Kongzi does not criticize any of the answers given by his disciples, but he approves only of the response given by Dian, declaring, "I am with Dian!" In light of what has been presented in this chapter, his approval not only shows his preference for what Dian suggests but also implies that the only way one could ever achieve the more grand aims expressed by the other three disciples is by ensuring that one takes the time and makes the effort to engage in activities like preparing and putting on the new clothes of the season, seeking out the company of young companions, bathing in the River Yi, drying off in the gentle breezes at the Altar of Rain, and then, together with them, returning home chanting.[21] In other words, while the Way calls on and inspires us to aim and work at the lofty goal of bringing peace to all the world, the path forward begins at our doorstep and can never be found apart from awareness, attentiveness, and care of and in the everyday.

7

CONCLUSION

I have offered brief introductions, analyses, and commentaries on six themes inspired by passages from the *Analects*. These reflections have come out of only one admittedly selective perspective on this marvelous text. They are of course "mine" but not wholly mine, for they are informed by more than thirty years of sustained study, discussion, teaching, and reflection upon this classic and its commentaries in Chinese, Korean, Japanese, and English, in the company of many cherished teachers, colleagues, and students, and in response to numerous interlocutors and respected adversaries. While a scholar of East Asian culture, philosophy, and religion, I have avoided deploying most of the technical vocabulary, format, and style found in these academic specialties in order to make the *Analects* and parts of its message more accessible to a broader audience, while at the same time providing some evidence and sketching arguments to support the claims I put forth. I have not said anything here that I am not prepared to support at greater length and in more detail as genuine concerns of this venerable classic and defend as eminently worthy topics of reflection for contemporary people. I have endeavored to present the issues I explore in a way that invites further reflection. Those who choose to take up such reflection will be joining in the Confucian tradition in the most important way anyone ever has or can, for they will be seeking to "revive what is past in order to understand what is new" (溫故而知新) (*Analects* 2.11). For those who wish to pursue these issues in further depth, the notes, work cited, and suggested further readings offer good places to start.

Some may raise an eyebrow, cast a scowl, or voice an objection to any study that seeks to demonstrate the contemporary relevance of a text with the complex history of the *Analects*. This can be a valid concern, but I have at least two things to say to those who hold strong versions of such a view. First, much of the complex history of the *Analects* is found in the rich tradition of commentaries on this text that can be found throughout East Asian cultures—and more recently in cultures beyond East Asia. Anyone who has taken the time and made the effort to study in a serious manner this vast treasury of creative and inspiring interpretations of the *Analects* will be awed, enchanted, intrigued, and delighted by the diversity, originality, and reverence shown in these works. The wisdom of the *Analects* is not something that has or could be handed down unchanged through time and across cultures; rather, the genius of this classic lies in its immense and protean power to inspire a series of innovative and profound insights concerning what it is to be a humane person and work for a flourishing and decent society. There is nothing trendy or exceptional about this effort, nor is it in any recognizable way an imposition of some Western model upon this venerable East Asian classic. In other words, to offer a reading of the *Analects* that seeks to show its *contemporary* relevance is to engage in the most *traditional* form of Confucian study. Second, some might insist that any introduction that succeeds in making the text accessible fails to convey its true and profound message. As a blanket statement, this either is trivially true or clearly false. It is true that no study could succeed in presenting "the true message" of the *Analects*—whatever that might mean. No interpretation could hope to represent *all* this text has meant, never mind all that it still shall mean, to those who read it. In any event, these have never been my goals or intent. My aim has been to introduce the text in a way that is accessible to interested readers but that leads them toward deep questions, questions that I expect neither they nor I will ever fully fathom but that both will find inviting, stimulating, and edifying.

The great Tang dynasty Confucian Han Yu 韓愈 (768–824) warned against taking up the wrong kinds of teachings—not because of any inherent danger in them per se but because they do not and cannot lead one to what is really profound and important. According to Han Yu, to seek the Dao through such teachings is "like sailing around in a closed off harbor or cut off lake with the hope of reaching the sea" (猶航斷港絕潢以望至於海也).[1] Like all great classics, the *Analects* raises many questions that have no final or definitive answers—questions like the meaning of human life, the nature of the debt we feel toward those who have helped shape our lives, how best to express friendship or love for another, or what precise form of society is best for us to construct and defend—but that richly repay serious engagement, discussion, and contemplation by every person and each generation. The value of such questions lies not only in the many wise, powerful, and productive answers that have and will be given to them but also in the quest they inspire each of us to undertake. This book is offered in order to facilitate such engagement, discussion, and contemplation, as an introduction to or point of departure for the deep and important questions that Kongzi explored in his life and work. I have sought to sketch several ideas found in the *Analects* that I regard as interesting and important, that have moved and inspired me for many years, and I offered some reasons to think that these teachings have much to say not only about the ancient Chinese and their later descendants, but also to all reflective human beings. If I may express my hope for this volume by extending Han Yu's metaphor, it is that this book can serve as a safe harbor and calm cove within which people can sail about, develop their skills, and gain their bearings, before setting off to explore the broad seas and far shores of the Confucian tradition and the more distant horizons of our common humanity.

NOTES

Notes to Preface

1. It is important to appreciate that the *Analects*, while the founding work of what became the Confucian tradition, is but one early work in a vast and complex tradition that is still very much alive and generating new works, ideas, and practices. Moreover, Confucianism is but one facet of rich and variegated cultures in China, Korea, Japan, and Vietnam.
2. Two earlier, highly influential short studies of the *Analects*, by Herbert Fingarette and Yu Dan, also have made the case for the contemporary relevance of its teachings, though in ways as different from one another as from the presentation I will offer here. See Herbert Fingarette, *Confucius: The Secular as Sacred* (New York: Harper and Row, 1972) and Yu Dan, *Confucius from the Heart: Ancient Wisdom for Today's World* (London: Macmillan, 2009).
3. In this respect I here am engaging in the kind of project that philosophers regularly undertake when seeking to draw lessons from traditional thinkers. For example, this is a widely followed approach to thinkers like Aristotle.

Notes to Introduction

1. For a thorough, though at times highly speculative, textual study of the *Analects*, see Bruce E. Brooks and Taeko A. Brooks, *The Original Analects*, Revised Second Edition (New York: Columbia University Press, 2001). For a work focused on Kongzi's thought and political activity, see Annping Chin, *Confucius: A Life of Thought and Politics* (New Haven, CT:

Yale University Press, 2008). For a historical treatment of Kongzi's life and later views of him, down to the present day, see Michael Nylan and Thomas Wilson, *Lives of Confucius: Civilization's Greatest Sage through the Ages* (New York: Doubleday, 2010). For a collection of essays on the text and its thought, see Bryan W. Van Norden, ed., *Confucius and the Analects: New Essays* (New York: Oxford University Press, 2002).

2. Confucianism has always been attractive to a small but dedicated group of Western intellectuals but in more recent years its appeal has grown much broader largely because of the work of a range of contemporary scholars who have presented it as an ethical and political philosophy or as a spiritual way of life. Examples of the former kind of work will be found throughout the coming chapters; some prominent examples of the latter kind of writing are: John H. Berthrong, *All Under Heaven: Transforming Paradigms in Confucian-Christian Dialogue* (Albany: State University of New York Press, 1994); Robert C. Neville, *Boston Confucianism Portable Tradition in the Late-Modern World* (Albany: State University of New York Press, 2000); Tu Weiming, *Centrality and Commonality: An Essay on Confucian Religiousness* (Albany: State University of New York Press, 1989); and Tu Weiming, ed., *The Living Tree: Changing Meaning of Being Chinese Today* (Palo Alto, CA: Stanford University Press, 1994).

3. Some contemporary scholars both within and outside of China have argued for political theories more closely related to traditional Confucianism, while others have argued that Kongzi was much more sympathetic to women than most people generally take him to be. For examples of the former, see Joseph Chan, "Democracy and Meritocracy: Toward a Confucian Perspective," *Journal of Chinese Philosophy* 34.2 (2007): 179–93; Daniel A. Bell, *Beyond Liberal Democracy: Political Thinking for an East Asian Context* (Princeton, NJ: Princeton University Press, 2006); Bai Tongdong, "A Mencian Version of Limited Democracy," *Res Publica* 14.1 (2008): 19–34; and Stephen C. Angle, *Contemporary Confucian Political Philosophy: Toward a Progressive Confucianism* (Cambridge: Polity Press, 2012). For examples of the latter, see Li Chenyang, "The Confucian Concept of Jen and the Feminist Ethics of Care: A Comparative Study," *Hypatia: A Journal of Feminist Philosophy* (January 1994): 70–89; Chan Sin Yee, "The Personal Is Political: Confucianism and Liberal Feminism," in *The Politics of Affective Relations* (Lanham, MD: Lexington, 2004): 97–118; and Li Hsiang Lisa Rosenlee, *Confucianism and Women: A Philosophical Interpretation* (Albany: State University of New York Press, 2007).

4. This line appears on the cover of this volume, along with a traditional picture of Kongzi. The inscription on the picture says, "An image of Kongzi, the first teacher, spreading his teachings."

5. Kongzi looked back to the culture of the Zhou dynasty (see *Analects* 3.14, 9.5, etc.) and later Confucians sought to revive Confucian "culture"

(see following note), but more often they spoke in terms of safeguarding and reviving the Way and being committed to the transmission of the Way. The Way meant on the one hand the various texts, rituals, and institutions of the golden age of the Zhou and on the other the trans-historical moral norms and principles that justified and informed the former and all later manifestations of the Way. For an interesting study of the role of culture in ethics, see Samuel Fleischacker, *The Ethics of Culture* (Ithaca and London: Cornell University Press, 1994). Fleischacker argues for the view that "cultures" are "authoritative traditions" and these provide the basis for ethical systems. While I have great sympathy with much that he has to say, I will treat traditions as narrower than cultures as this has always been true of Confucianism as a tradition within Chinese (Korean, Japanese, Vietnamese, etc.) culture.

6. In certain periods, especially when the Chinese have felt their cultural identity threatened, this aspect of the Confucian tradition became even more pronounced and explicit. For a study that explores this phenomenon in an exceptionally insightful way, see Peter Bol, *"This Culture of Ours": Intellectual Transitions in T'ang and Sung China* (Stanford, CA: Stanford University Press, 1992). One can make a good case that our current age is another period where this aspect of the Confucian tradition is gaining particular prominence and poignancy within Chinese and other East Asian societies.

7. For Kierkegaard's views on the self, see his *Sickness Unto Death*, trans. by Howard V. Hong and Edna H. Hong (Princeton, NJ: Princeton University Press, 1980). Sartre's famous distinction between *être-en-soi* ("being-in-itself") versus *être-pour-soi* ("being-for-itself") can be found in his *Being and Nothingness: An Essay in Phenomenological Ontology*, trans. by Hazel E. Barnes (New York: Pocket Press, 1978).

8. Sartre argues that what we are is largely what we, as individuals, choose to be, but Kierkegaard agrees with Confucians that we don't determine our own nature; that is something God alone determines. Most traditional Confucians, from Kongzi, Mengzi (391–308 BCE), and Xunzi (310–219 BCE) to Zhu Xi (1130–1200 CE) and Wang Yangming (1472–1529 CE), share such a view, since they all believe the right human culture expresses a heavenly conferred human nature.

9. Ludwig Wittgenstein made similar points about language in general in his book *Philosophical Investigations*, trans. by William H. Brenner (Albany: State University of New York Press, 1999); and Hilary Putnam put this point in terms of meanings not being in our heads in his "Meaning and Reference," *The Journal of Philosophy* 70–19 (1973): 699–711.

10. In the modern Western tradition, some philosophers have explored a similar line of thought about the evaluation of desires. For example, see Charles Taylor, "What Is Human Agency?" in *Human Agency and Language: Philosophical Papers 1* (Cambridge: Cambridge University

Press, 1990): 15–44; and Harry G. Frankfurt, "The Freedom of the Will and the Concept of a Person," *The Journal of Philosophy* 68.1 (1971): 5–20.

11. By "organically related," I mean that one cannot separate one's full happiness from the happiness of others; the latter is a constitutive part of the former. For my understanding of early Confucian views on-happiness, see my "Happiness in Early Chinese Thought," in Ilona Boniwell and Susan David, eds., *Oxford Handbook of Happiness* (Oxford, England: Oxford University Press, 2012).

12. For the importance of rituals in Confucianism, see Fingarette, *Confucius: The Secular as Sacred*, and Justin Tiwald and T.C. Kline III, eds., *Ritual and Religion in the Xunzi* (Albany: State University of New York Press, 2014). For a collection of contemporary essays on the philosophical dimensions of ritual, see Kevin Schilbrack, ed., *Thinking Through Rituals: Philosophical Perspectives* (New York: Routledge, 2004). For the importance of texts and commentaries, see John B. Henderson, *Scripture, Canon, and Commentary*, (Princeton, NJ: Princeton University Press, 1991); Ch'un-chieh Huang, *Mencian Hermeneutics: A History of Interpretations in China* (New Brunswick, NJ: Transaction Publishers, 2001); and John Makeham, *Transmitters and Creators: Chinese Commentators and Commentaries on the Analects* (Harvard East Asian Monographs; Cambridge, MA: Harvard University Asia Center, 2004).

13. For a splendid collection of essays on the general topic of the revival of traditional religion in contemporary China, see *China Perspectives*, Number 4 (2009). For an article in this collection particularly pertinent to the revival of Confucian ritual, see Sébastien Billioud and Joël Thoraval, "*Lijiao*: The Return of Ceremonies Honouring Confucius in Mainland China," pp. 82–100.

14. Of course, as we will discuss later in this chapter, if they do not agree with their country's decision to go to war, such occasions can generate songs of protest and calls for peace.

15. For a contemporary Confucian philosopher who takes a particular conception of the family as foundational for a range of ethical, social, and political issues, see Fan Ruiping, *Reconstructionist Confucianism: Rethinking Morality after the West* (Dordrecht; New York: Springer, 2010).

16. For an informative and insightful study exploring this issue in the Western tradition, see Jeffrey Blustein, *Parents and Children: The Ethics of the Family* (New York: Oxford University Press, 1982).

17. For an incisive study of many of the implications such a view has for our understanding the ethical dimensions of early childhood education and social policies that effectively support good outcomes, see Erin M. Cline, "Confucian Ethics, Public Policy, and the Nurse-Family Partnership," *Dao: A Journal of Comparative Philosophy* 11.3 (2012): 337–56.

18. As we will see in this chapter, this and other features of families were analyzed with great insight by the Ming dynasty Confucian, Li Zhi (1527–1602 CE).

Notes to Chapter 1

1. For revealing discussions of the nature and values of tradition, see Edward Shils, *Tradition* (Chicago: University of Chicago Press, 1981) and Jaroslav Pelikan, *The Vindication of Tradition: The 1983 Jefferson Lecture in the Humanities* (New Haven, CT: Yale University Press, 1989). Shils offers one of the most widely invoked and accepted definitions of tradition as "anything which is transmitted or handed down from the past to the present" (*Tradition*, p. 12). As we shall see, this works well for a general sense of the Confucian tradition.

2. For a splendid study that argues much the same point about social institutions, see Robert Bellah, Richard Madsen, William M. Sullivan, Ann Swidler, and Steven M. Tipton, *The Good Society* (New York: Vintage Books, 1992), especially the Introduction. See also Robert Bellah, Richard Madsen, William M. Sullivan, Ann Swidler, and Steven M. Tipton, *Habits of the Heart: Individualism and Commitment in American Life* (New York: Harper and Row, 1985).

3. *The Vindication of Tradition*, p. 65.

4. In a number of spectacular works, Alasdair MacIntyre has argued that traditions are essential not only for ethics but rationality itself. See his *After Virtue*, Second Edition (Notre Dame, IN: University of Notre Dame Press, 1984); *Whose Justice? Which Rationality?* (Notre Dame, IN: University of Notre Dame Press, 1988); and *Three Rival Versions of Moral Enquiry: Encyclopedia, Genealogy, and Tradition* (Notre Dame, IN: University of Notre Dame Press, 1990). For a splendid and powerful analysis of the role of tradition in democracy, see Jeffrey Stout, *Democracy and Tradition* (Princeton, NJ: Princeton University Press, 2004).

5. For the senses in which social phenomena can be understood as facts about the world, see John Searle, *The Construction of Social Reality* (New York: The Free Press, 1995) and Hilary Putnam, *Meaning and the Moral Sciences* (London: Routledge and Kegan Paul, 1978).

6. For a decisive refutation of such narrow conceptions of rational interest, see Amartya K. Sen, "Rational Fools: A Critique of the Behavioral Foundations of Economic Theory," *Philosophy and Public Affairs*, 6.4 (1977): 317–44.

7. For a study that treats many of the modern challenges to Christian traditionalism, see John Herman Randall, *The Making of the Modern Mind: A Survey of the Intellectual Background of the Present Age*, Reprint (New York: Columbia University Press, 1976). For a seminal study

that argues Confucianism ran aground on the shores of modernity, see Joseph R. Levenson, *Confucian China and Its Modern Fate: A Trilogy* (Berkeley: University of California Press, 1965). For modern Chinese criticisms of Confucius, see Kam Louie, *Critiques of Confucius in Contemporary China* (Hong Kong: Chinese University Press, 1980).

8. Steven Pinker has argued persuasively that the general level of violence, of just about every kind, has declined worldwide because of changes in culture and technology that support and encourage greater cooperation and peace. See his *The Better Angels of Our Nature: Why Violence Has Declined* (New York: Viking Penguin, 2011). Thanks to Owen Flanagan for noting the relevance of Pinker's work to the question of traditions.

9. From a letter Zhang wrote to Sun Xingyan 孫星衍 in 1797. For a discussion of this passage and the notion of temporal provincialism, see my "Lessons from the Past: Zhang Xuecheng and the Ethical Dimensions of History," *Dao: A Journal of Comparative Philosophy*, 8.2 (June 2009): 189–203. Zhang's view is not unlike that of Richard Rorty. See Richard Rorty, "Cosmopolitanism without Emancipation: A Response to Jean-Francois Lyotard," in Richard Rorty, *Objectivity, Relativism and Truth* (Cambridge: Cambridge University Press, 1991): 211–22. Thanks to Owen Flanagan for pointing this out to me.

10. The Duke of Zhou was exemplary for putting the good of the state before his own personal welfare. A failure to keep in one's heart and mind such exemplary people from within one's tradition is a sign of ethical drift.

11. Johann Wolfgang von Goethe, *Faust*, lines 682–3.

12. The relatively low social and economic status of teachers in modern liberal societies is largely a result of a general failure to understand the roles tradition plays in educating and shaping human beings. Thanks to Michael R. Slater for bringing this implication to my attention.

13. Love of learning is a theme throughout the *Analects*; see 1.14, 6.3, 8.13, 8.15, 11.7, 17.7, and 19.5.

14. Even in traditions that place a very high premium on novelty, such as pop music and modern art, participants and admirers tend not to see the value of the new as being to the detriment of the old. Few think the value of a recently developed "new sound" is in any way a function of how poor past pop music was. Most successful rock musicians admire the old folk and blues musicians, even as they work to distinguish their sound from these and other prior and contemporary artists. Thanks for Justin Tiwald and Melanie J. Dorson for suggesting this line of thought.

15. For a revealing discussion of this aspect of Xunzi's ethical philosophy, see chapter 5 of T.C. Kline III, *Ethics and Tradition in the* Xunzi (Ph.D. dissertation, Stanford University, 1998): 205–41.

16. Wynton Marsalis offers a contemporary example of someone who shares this particular sensibility in regard to his art. See Wynton Marsalis and Selwyn Seyfu Hinds, *To a Young Jazz Musician: Letters from the Road* (New York: Random House, 2004).

17. Many modern Western intellectuals and in recent years more than a few East Asian intellectuals live within these kinds of tensions. Anglo-American philosophers offer a particularly acute example: their embrace of natural science as the primary model for how to do philosophy leaves them with a severe challenge to justify their study of the history of their discipline. If, like natural science, philosophy is about the latest and best theories, why study the past? Physicists do physics; they don't offer classes in the history of physics.

18. Charles Taylor makes a related case against the vacuous and futile search for authenticity based on a bare notion of choice. We can't find meaning in choice alone, no matter how much emotion we inject into it. Choices have meaning only against a background of and in conversation with existing traditions of value. See Charles Taylor, *The Ethics of Authenticity* (Cambridge, MA: Harvard University Press, 1991).

19. Some commentators take Kongzi's declaration to be primarily an expression of profound humility. I follow those who understand it more at face value. This is not to deny that his remark expresses proper humility nor should this interpretation be taken as denying the creative role selection, presentation, and explication can play in acts of transmission.

20. Liam Murphy and Thomas Nagel refer to the idea that we create all the wealth we own as "the myth of ownership." See Liam Murphy and Thomas Nagel, *The Myth of Ownership: Taxes and Justice* (New York: Oxford University Press, 2002). For a revealing discussion of how such ideas can form into grand narratives about the self, see Owen Flanagan, "Moral Science? Still Metaphysical After All These Years," in *Personality, Identity and Character: Explorations in Moral Psychology,* ed. Darcia Narvaez and Daniel K. Lapsley (New York: Cambridge University Press, 2009): 69–71.

21. In his 1676 letter to his rival Robert Hooke, Newton declared, "What Descartes did was a good step. You have added much several ways, and especially in taking the colours of thin plates into philosophical consideration. If I have seen a little further it is by standing on the shoulders of Giants." http://en.wikipedia.org/wiki/Standing_on_the_shoulders_of_giants

22. In much the same way, human beings are the only creatures who have history in the sense of a continuing story of their past. All creatures are parts of history in the broadest sense, but none, save us, has *history*.

Notes to Chapter 2

1. For an insightful discussion of this issue, see Stephen Darwall's review article, "The Invention of Autonomy," *European Journal of Philosophy* 7.3 (1999): 339–50.

2. Hugo Grotius, *The Laws of War and Peace,* trans. by Francis W. Kelsey (New York: Carnegie Endowment for International Peace, 1925).

3. Mary Midgley offers a spirited philosophical challenge to this kind of view in her work *The Solitary Self: Darwin and the Selfish Gene* (Durham, England: Acumen, 2010) and overwhelming evidence against such a view can be found from the fields of psychology, evolutionary biology, neuroscience, and animal ethnography. For example, see C.D. Batson, "Prosocial Motivation: Is It Ever Truly Altruistic?" in *Advances in Experimental Social Psychology,* Volume 20, ed. L. Berkowitz (New York: Academic Press, 1987): 65–122; Martin L. Hoffman, *Empathy and Moral Development: Implications for Caring and Justice,* Reprint (New York: Cambridge University Press, 2007); Elliot Sober and David Sloan Wilson, *Unto Others: The Evolution and Psychology of Unselfish Behavior,* (Cambridge, MA: Harvard University Press, 1998); Antonio Damasio, *Descartes' Error: Emotion, Reason, and the Human Brain,* Revised Second Edition (New York: Penguin Books, 2005); and Frans de Waal, *The Age of Empathy: Nature's Lessons for a Kinder Society* (New York: Harmony Books, 2009).

4. For a poignant and revealing exploration of this tension in contemporary American life from a social scientific perspective, see Bellah et al., *Habits of the Heart.*

5. Susan Wolf offers a scathing attack on the very notion of being a moral saint in her seminal essay "Moral Saints," *The Journal of Philosophy* 79.8 (August 1982): 419–39. Robert Adams offers a penetrating rejoinder to her account in his "Saints," *The Journal of Philosophy* 81.7 (July 1984): 392–401. Peter Singer's ethical view does place extremely high demands on people, though he insists that these are not as strong as many people claim they are. For his view, see Peter Singer, "Famine, Affluence, and Morality," *Philosophy and Public Affairs* 1.3 (1972): 229–43. For an analysis of his view as a call to sainthood, see the Introduction to Rebecca Walker and Philip J. Ivanhoe, eds., *Working Virtue: Virtue Ethics and Contemporary Moral Problems* (New York: Oxford University Press, 2007): 34.

6. For a revealing discussion of this issue, see Samuel Scheffler, *Human Morality* (New York: Oxford University Press, 1992). See especially chapter two.

7. This apparent paradox was first mentioned by Henry Sidgwick (1838–1900) in his *The Methods of Ethics,* Seventh Edition (Indianapolis, IN: Hackett Publishing Company, 1981).

8. Many of Dickens's works also both depict and elicit in their readers the kind of personal transformation I discuss here; *Oliver Twist* is another excellent example.

9. For a version of this kind of dilemma, see Michael Stocker, "The Schizophrenia of Modern Ethical Theories," in Roger Crisp and Michael Slote, eds. *Virtue Ethics* (New York: Oxford University Press, 1998): 66–78.

10. For a remarkable account of our complex relationship to the rest of the living world, see Edwin O. Wilson, *Biophilia* (Cambridge, MA: Harvard University Press, 1984).

11. For a more thorough discussion of this aspect of the Confucian view, see my "Happiness in Early Chinese Thought."

12. Mengzi was the first well-known and influential follower of Kongzi. His interpretation of Kongzi's philosophy played a commanding role in the shape and direction of later "neo-Confucian" tradition. Because of his importance within the Confucian tradition, Mengzi often is referred to as the "second sage" (*yasheng* 亞聖). For introductions to his thought, see Kwong-loi Shun, *Mencius and Early Chinese Thought* (Stanford, CA: Stanford University Press, 1997); and Xiusheng Liu and Philip J. Ivanhoe, eds., *Essays on the Moral Philosophy of Mengzi* (Indianapolis, IN: Hackett Publishing, 2002).

13. While not as highly regarded within the later Confucian orthodoxy as Mengzi, Xunzi is the most philosophically sophisticated Confucian of the classical period and had tremendous influence on later Chinese and East Asian philosophy. For introductions to his thought, see, Paul Goldin, *Rituals of the Way* (LaSalle, IL: Open Court Press, 1999); Eric L. Hutton, *Virtue and Reason in Xunzi* (Ph.D. dissertation, Stanford University, 2001); and T.C. Kline III and Philip J. Ivanhoe, eds., *Virtue, Nature and Agency in the Xunzi* (Indianapolis, IN: Hackett Publishing Company, 2000). For an excellent comparison of their views and those of two important Western philosophers, see Eric Schwitzgebel, "Human Nature and Moral Development in Mencius, Xunzi, Hobbes, and Rousseau," *History of Philosophy Quarterly* 24 (2007): 147–68.

14. See chapter 27, the "Great Compendium" (*Dalue* 大略), of the *Xunzi*. For the quotation in the *Analects* see *Analects* 1.15.

15. For a more thorough and detailed discussion of these different expressions of the Confucian vision, see my *Confucian Moral Self Cultivation*, Revised Second Edition (Indianapolis, IN: Hackett Publishing Company, 2006).

16. He does use vegetative metaphors to discuss some of the threats to and errors associated with self-cultivation. For a discussion of these and the Mengzi's use of agricultural versus vegetative metaphors, see my *Ethics in the Confucian Tradition: The Thought of Mengzi and Wang*

Yangming, Revised Second Edition (Indianapolis, IN: Hackett Publishing Company, 2002): 43–4, 64, 90–95.

17. In a similar way, almost nothing we who live in modern industrial societies, eat is wholly natural—not even what you might buy in the "natural food" section. The animals, vegetables, fruits, nuts etc. we consume are the result of thousands of years of sustained and careful human manipulation aimed at producing more hearty, delicious, and visually appealing food.

18. Owen Flanagan has made a compelling case for what he calls "minimal psychological realism" as a constraint upon moral theorizing. See especially chapter two of his *Varieties of Moral Personality: Ethics and Psychological Realism* (Cambridge, MA: Harvard University Press, 1991).

19. In the later Confucian tradition, the idea of being connected with other people, creatures, and things came to be expressed in terms of the ideal of seeing oneself as "one" with the world. One of the most common and influential ways of expressing this ideal was through the metaphor of "being one body with heaven, earth, and the myriad creatures" (天地萬物為一體). For an analysis of this idea and its contemporary significance, see David W. Tien, "Oneness and Self-Centeredness in the Moral Psychology of Wang Yangming," *Journal of Religious Ethics* 40.1 (2012): 52–71; and my "Senses and Values of Oneness" in *The Philosophical Challenge from China,* ed. Brian Bruya (Cambridge, MA: MIT Press, 2014).

Notes to Chapter 3

1. For a revealing discussion of this aspect of early Confucianism, see Stephen Wilson, "Conformity, Individuality, and the Nature of Virtue: A Classical Confucian Contribution to Contemporary Ethical Reflection," in *Confucius and the Analects: New Essays,* ed. Bryan W. Van Norden (New York: Oxford University Press, 2001): 94–115.

2. Herbert Fingarette was the first to use the example of shaking hands to explicate and draw attention to Confucian ritual in his seminal work *Confucius: The Secular as Sacred*. See especially pages 9–10.

3. Relying on the analogy of theatrical performance, Erving Goffman has produced a profound account of how human beings in social situations work to present themselves, their actions, and activities in ways that inform and shape the interpretations and impressions others form. See his *The Presentation of Self in Everyday Life* (New York: Anchor Books, 1959).

4. See for example Charles Taylor's essay "Self Interpreting Animals" in *Human Agency and Language: Philosophical Papers* (Cambridge: Cambridge University Press, 1985): 45–76; and his book *Sources of the Self:*

The Making of Modern Identity (Cambridge, MA: Harvard University Press, 1989).

5. Joel J. Kupperman has written revealingly about the ways in which Kongzi is concerned with *style* as an important aspect of the good life. See Kupperman, "Naturalness Revisited: Why Western Philosophers Should Study Confucius," in *Confucius and the* Analects: *New Essays*, ed. Bryan W. Van Norden (New York: Oxford University Press, 2002): 39–52. See also Amy Olberding, "Ascending the Hall: Style and Moral Improvement in the *Analects*," *Philosophy East and West* 59.4 (October 2009): 503–22.

6. Wittgenstein presents this argument in §243 of his book *Philosophical Investigations*.

7. Recently, Robert B. Brandom has presented a careful, thorough, and compelling case that human linguistic activity is fundamentally a form of social practice. See his *Making It Explicit: Reasoning, Representing, and Discursive Commitment* (Cambridge, MA: Harvard University Press, 1994).

8. For a remarkable account of how emotions and the entire body are intimately involved in human thought, see Antonio Damasio, *Descartes' Error: Emotion, Reason, and the Human Brain* (New York: Penguin Books, 1994).

9. See Brad K. Wilburn, "Moral Self-Improvement," in *Moral Cultivation: Essays on the Development of Character and Virtue*, ed. Brad K. Wilburn (Lanham, MD: Lexington Books, 2007): 71–86.

10. John Rawls, *A Theory of Justice* (Cambridge, MA: The Belknap Press, 1971).

11. This part of his analysis bears remarkable similarities and could have been strengthened by Confucian views. For revealing comparative studies of Rawls and Kongzi, see Erin M. Cline, "Two Senses of Justice: Confucianism, Rawls, and Comparative Political Philosophy," *Dao: A Journal of Comparative Philosophy* 6:4 (Winter 2007): 361–81; and *Confucius, Rawls, and the Sense of Justice* (New York: Fordham University Press, 2013).

12. My claim should not be understood as saying that a sense of justice as fairness does not also depend on other kinds of social rituals, norms, and practices, but I do intend to imply that it is our actual *practices* and *social expectations* rather than some theory or innate inclination, that first generate our sense of fairness. For a marvelous anthology exploring the many ethical dimensions of sport, see William J. Morgan, ed., *Ethics in Sport*, Second Edition (Champaign, IL: Human Kinetics, 2007).

13. Such rituals sometimes are present, when the game is played in a more serious, formal setting (e.g., a professional chess match).

14. One exception to this generalization, which I owe to Michael R. Slater, is golf, in which players are expected to keep track of, enforce, and

report any violation of the rules they might commit. An even more dramatic and elaborate exception is Ultimate Frisbee, which in the United States is now a regular inter-collegiate sport and is played at both the high school and professional levels. Ultimate Frisbee tournaments are self-refereed and after each game, players from each team rate the other team on their "spirit" and nominate a single player from the opposing team who displays the "best spirit." Undoubtedly, this is a game whose practices Kongzi would endorse! Compare the passage on archery discussed in the chapter text. Thanks to Owen Flanagan for this example.

15. The importance of archery can be seen not only in philosophical texts like the *Analects* and *Mengzi* but also in ritual texts such as the *"Book of Rites"* (*Liji* 禮記) and literary texts such as the *Book of Odes*. For example, see "The Meaning of the Archery Ceremony" (*She yi* 射義) and "The Game of Pitch Pot" (*tou hu* 投壺) chapters in the former, and the poem "When the Guests Arrive" (*bin zhi chu yan* 賓之初筵) in the latter (*Mao #* 220).

16. Receiving a call by identifying oneself is a practice that, unfortunately, should probably be abandoned because of concerns about personal safety. Thanks to James F. Peterman for bringing up this point.

17. The one general exception to this lack of ritual attention is savvy businesses which discovered long ago and know well that proper phone etiquette results in much better business outcomes.

18. While there are technological challenges to the use of cell phones on aircraft all of these can be addressed with current technology. (If the signal were not blocked, you could simply Skype on airlines that provide Wi-Fi service.) The primary reason most airlines have continued the ban on cell phones is customer resistance to their use. Representative Peter Defazio (D-Oregon) has sponsored a bill in the U.S. Congress to ban all cell phone use on commercial airplanes called the Halting Airplane Noise to Give Us Peace Act (HANG UP). For the bill, see http://thomas.loc.gov/cgi-bin/query/z?c110:H.R.5788. The same policy of banning cell phone use is now in force on many trains as well, on which "quiet" carriages block all cell phone signals.

19. Thanks to Owen Flanagan for this example.

20. In a recent meeting on reviving Confucian ritual in China, the contemporary Confucian thinker Jiang Qing 蔣庆 made a similar point about the relative hygienic value of traditional forms of salutation. I was told this in a personal communication from Daniel A. Bell.

21. The extent to which casual hand-to-hand contact spreads disease is clear from the fact that hand washing is the most important step people can take to stop the spread of disease. According to the United States *Centers of Disease Control and Prevention* (*CDC*), "Hand washing is the single most important means of preventing the spread of infection" (http://www.cdc.gov/).

22. Daniel Bell explores the ways in which bowing and ritual in general in East Asian societies manifest a greater acceptance of social inequality. I agree, though am less inclined to endorse or encourage this feature of the practice. See his "Hierarchical Rituals for Egalitarian Societies" in Daniel A. Bell, *China's New Confucianism: Politics and Everyday Life in a Changing Society* (Princeton, NJ: Princeton University Press, 2008): 38–55.

23. The closest correlate to this Chinese ritual in the West is found in the military practice of saluting, which enjoys many of the advantages described above. The Chinese practice, though, does not incorporate the requirement that one salute all and only *officers* (something enlisted personnel regularly ignore once no longer on active duty) and in this respect is more universal and egalitarian.

24. For a revealing analysis of these aspects of Confucian ritual, which includes a careful analysis of the passage quoted below, see Kwong-loi Shun, "*Jen* and *Li* in the Analects," in *Confucius and the* Analects*: New Essays,* ed. Bryan W. Van Norden (New York: Oxford University Press, 2001): 53–72. For a contemporary example of how innovating and adhering to a simple ritual can alter and enhance many lives, see John Kralik, *365 Thank Yous: The Year a Simple Act of Daily Gratitude Changed My Life* (New York: Hyperion Books, 2010).

Notes to Chapter 4

1. Johann Gottfried Herder saw all meaningful human activity as arising from cultures or in his terms different *Volk*. This led him to collect and comment upon folk songs (a term he coined), and his collection was later published as *Voices of the People in Their Songs* (*Stimmen der Völker in ihren Liedern*, 1773). His views inspired Jacob and Wilhelm Grimm to collect German folk tales, and their work is known today under the popular title of *Grimms' Fairy Tales*.

2. In modern, pluralistic societies it might be less common to discover a dominant consensus in music or any other medium of expression. That is an empirical issue and will vary with time and circumstance. Even if we find less consensus and greater diversity, in more or less homogenous societies, this in itself could be important and revealing. Thanks to Jennifer D. White for raising this issue.

3. See also the opening paragraphs of the "Explaining the Classics" (*Jingjie* 經解) chapter of the *Book of Rites* and the "Great Preface" (*Daxu* 大序) to the *Book of Odes*.

4. The Taliban tried to ban all music in Afghanistan but thus far have failed miserably to do so.

5. While I here draw upon important features of the metaphor of a symphony, which traditional Confucians did in fact endorse, it is important

to point out how this metaphor has been misunderstood by some scholars and misused by authoritarian leaders, especially in regard to the notion of harmony. Too briefly put, traditional Confucians did not invoke this metaphor to imply that everyone should simply play her part *as written* in some assigned score or that everyone in the symphony (i.e., the members of society) should follow the direction of some conductor (i.e., leader). In fact the early Confucian notion of harmony works in the opposite direction: a good leader is to find ways to bring together different and distinct views just as a great cook counterbalances and blends different tastes or a great composer harmonizes different sounds. Harmony *requires* the preservation of diversity and contrast.

6. This relationship is not just casual or accidental as seen in expressions such as "virtuous words" (lit. "virtuous sounds," *de yin* 德音), which appears in the *Book of Odes* about a dozen times. Thanks to Justin Tiwald for pointing this out. For a description and analysis of early Chinese notions about virtue, see my "The Concept of *De* ('Virtue') in the *Laozi*," in *Religious and Philosophical Aspects of the Laozi*, ed. Mark Csikszentmihalyi and Philip J. Ivanhoe (Albany: State University of New York Press, 1999): 239–57.

7. Of course, the particular effect and impact a given piece of music will have is influenced by cultural and environmental factors as well.

8. See chapter 20 of the *Xunzi*, "On Music" (*Yuelun* 樂論), where the line appears twice. It also appears in the "Record of Music" chapter of the *Book of Rites*.

9. This offers but one respect in which Kongzi's views on music differ from those of Plato. The latter thought that the beautiful and the good cannot be separated in the way that Kongzi here suggests. Incidentally, since we do not possess any musical scores from this period of Chinese history, we do not know what either the Wu or Shao sounded like, though we do have a good idea of the kinds of instruments upon which they were played and the kinds of performances that accompanied them. Thanks to Daniel A. Bell for discussing these and related issues with me.

10. For Kongzi's concern about glib talkers, see *Analects* 1.3, 15.11, 17.15, etc. For the Daoist view, see the *Daodejing*, chapters 23, 45, 56, 78, 81.

11. David S. Nivison offers a fascinating account of how this distrust of oratorical skill might reflect Kongzi's attempt to distinguish his conception of "complete virtue" (*ren* 仁) (later in the tradition, often the specific virtue of "benevolence") from earlier more aristocratic conceptions, which tended to focus on fineness and nobility of appearance or presentation as opposed to issues of character. Part of Nivison's argument relies on the graphic and phonetic similarity between the characters for *ren* and "eloquence" (*ning* 佞), which in Kongzi's time were pronounced something like **nien* and **nieng* respectively. See "The Classic Philosophical Writings," in *The Cambridge History of Ancient China:*

From the Origins of Civilization to 221 B.C., ed. Michael Loewe and Edward L. Shaughnessy (New York: Cambridge University Press, 1999): 751–2.

12. This line of reasoning could be extended to modern visual media such as film and television. The implication is that these modern forms of art represent powerful methods of moving others easily, swiftly, and profoundly. Given these qualities, they hold great potential for mischief as well as good. Leni Riefenstall's *Triumph of the Will* (1935) and *Olympia* (1938) offer good examples of the danger of film, while *Casablanca* and Al Gore's *An Inconvenient Truth* are excellent examples of its potential for good.

13. Hanfeizi, a political realist or Legalist thinker, also warned against the power of glib speakers and instead advocated reliance upon clearly written essays. Perhaps, though, this had much to do with the fact that he stuttered quite severely. The Mohists, early competitors of the Confucians, opposed literary eloquence, because they thought it contributed nothing to good reasoning and only served to obscure poor arguments.

14. For a splendid account of how evolution has shaped our attitudes toward Nature, see E.O. Wilson, *Biophilia*. For an anthology that applies these insights to various social and cultural phenomena, see, Stephen R. Kellert and Edward O. Wilson, eds., *The Biophilia Hypothesis,* Reprint (Washington, D.C.: Island Press, 1995).

15. For a revealing study of the most popular of all Chinese revolutionary operas, which does a splendid job not only of describing its blending of music and dance but also of showing how such works picked up and redeployed traditional folk songs and themes, see Joys H.Y. Cheung, "'The North Wind Blows': Sounding Bitterness in *The White-Haired Girl,* a Communist Political Ritual," in *Reading Chinese Music and Beyond*, ed. Joys H.Y. Cheung and King Chun Wong (Hong Kong: Chinese Civilization Centre, City University of Hong Kong, 2010): 87–199.

16. Such ideas, properly qualified, find confirmation in recent work in psychology and cognitive science. For example, see William Forde Thompson, *Music, Thought, and Feeling: Understanding the Psychology of Music* (New York: Oxford University Press, 2008).

17. Kongzi's conception of music could be strengthened by the view advanced by Susanne Langer. She argues that music is not helpfully thought of as possessing the semantic content or grammar of a language or simply as the pure expression of emotion. Music is *symbolic* in both nature and function. See Susanne K. Langer, *Philosophy in a New Key: A Study in the Symbolism of Reason, Rite, and Art* (New York: New American Library, 1951): 174–208. Another revealing study of the nature and ethical dimensions of music is Kathleen M. Higgins, *The Music of Our Lives* (Philadelphia: Temple University Press, 1991).

Higgins has an insightful essay on music in Confucianism as well: "Music in Confucian and Neo-Confucian Philosophy," *International Philosophical Quarterly* 20.4 (December 1980): 433–51.

18. Frans de Waal describes some of the evidence for such claims in his *The Age of Empathy: Nature's Lessons for a Kinder Society* (New York: Harmony Books, 2009): 63–5, noting that the power of music to achieve such ends is found in other species as well as among human beings.

19. Some rock performers as well as other musicians have focused their music and its power toward noble ends such as helping to relieve hunger or poverty or fighting AIDS. Mengzi would encourage them to *rock on*; Kongzi would see them as manifesting the purpose if not the full form of the Dao.

20. As noted above, Mengzi makes a similar point about the ability of shared musical experience to inculcate greater social solidarity and as a bridge toward wider ethical feelings.

21. The ways in and extent to which contemporary music in modern industrialized cultures is shaped, packaged, and marketed by the music industry makes the diagnostic function of music less reliable and accurate as a gauge of what is going on spontaneously in these societies. Nevertheless, one can see a case for arguing that despite the immense power and influence of the music industry, genuine popular sentiment and style have a way of breaking through and expressing themselves. For various reasons, in societies like contemporary China, the local music scene remains an accurate and revealing diagnostic for gauging popular sentiments.

22. Allan Bloom offered a scathing critique of rock music in general and the Rolling Stones in particular in his widely read and discussed book *The Closing of the American Mind* (New York: Simon & Schuster, 1987). A more sophisticated criticism of popular music can be found in Roger Scruton, *The Aesthetics of Music* (New York: Oxford University Press, 1999).

23. When the Rolling Stones appeared on the same show, on 15 January 1967, they were asked and agreed to substitute the line "Let's spend *some time* together" for the more suggestive "Let's spend *the night* together." Expressing his dissent regarding this concession, Mick Jagger made a point of rolling his eyes in disbelief every time he sang the altered refrain.

24. These fears about the seductive power of music recall the legend of the Pied Piper of Hamelin, who led the children of the village of Hamelin away through the power of his flute.

Notes to Chapter 5

1. For a discussion of filial piety as a modern virtue, see my "Filial Piety as a Virtue," in Rebecca Walker and Philip J. Ivanhoe, eds., *Working Virtue: Virtue Ethics and Contemporary Moral Problems*, pp. 297–312,

2. I thank Paul Kjellberg for very insightful help in thinking through the issues explored in this section.

3. This general point is the central theme of Alasdair MacIntyre's splendid book *Dependent Rational Animals: Why Human Beings Need the Virtues* (Chicago: Open Court, 1999). As much as I admire this work, it also offers an excellent example of a project that would have benefitted tremendously from a sophisticated engagement with Confucianism

4. For a general study of the lives of women in early China, which contains helpful discussions of Mengzi's mother, see Lisa Raphals, *Sharing the Light: Representations of Women and Virtue in Early China* (Albany: State University of New York Press, 1998). For a comprehensive collection of sources on women in traditional Chinese thought and culture, see Robin R. Wang, ed., *Images of Women in Chinese Thought and Culture: Writings from the Pre-Qin Period to the Song Dynasty* (Indianapolis, IN: Hackett Publishing Company, 2003).

5. For an exploration of this latter issue, see Joshua Cohen, "Okin on Justice, Gender, and Family," *Canadian Journal of Philosophy* 22.2 (1992): 263–86.

6. I analyze the role of Heaven in early Confucian ethics in my "Heaven as a Source for Ethical Warrant in Early Confucianism," *Dao: A Journal of Comparative Philosophy*, 6.3 (2007): 211–20.

7. Frans de Waal makes this point with particularly poignancy in his *The Age of Empathy*, for example on pages 20–22, noting that human families bear remarkable similarities to the kin groups and social organization of many other pack animals. Of course, as de Waal notes as well, this does not mean it is illegitimate to use thought-experiments of hypothetical contracting to illustrate important philosophical points.

8. A number of thinkers, such as Plato, certain Marxists, and some in the Israeli Kibbutz movement, have argued that we abandon this age-old human practice and raise children collectively. Such recommendations have remained philosophical phantasies or failed miserably when put into practice.

9. The love and commitment married couples without children have for one another and for their adult parents and other relatives offers a separate but related set of reasons to give families special status within society, but I will not explore this aspect of family life here. Thanks to Daniel A. Bell for raising this issue.

10. For a revealing analysis of the public-private debate, its relationship to families, and its implications for women, see Carole Patemen, *The Disorder of Women: Democracy, Feminism, and Political Theory* (Cambridge: Polity Press 1989).

11. For those interested in pursuing these issues further, the classic work on this topic is Susan Moller Okin, *Justice, Gender, and the Family* (New York: Basic Books, 1989).

12. Compare the discussion of schizophrenia and the reference to the work of Michael Stocker, "The Schizophrenia of Modern Ethical Theories,"

13. See Pauline Chen Lee, "Li Zhi and John Stuart Mill: A Confucian Feminist Critique of Liberal Feminism," in *The Sage and the Second Sex: Confucianism, Ethics, and Gender*, ed. Li Chenyang (Chicago: Open Court Press, 2000): 113–32.

14. While traditional Confucianism appreciated the roles emotions play in moral perception, reflection, and judgment and avoided the kind of strict division between public and private that animates much political philosophy in the West, they did develop essentialized conceptions of human nature that supported unequal, gendered conceptions of men's and women's proper work. They thereby undermined what I regard as their more accurate and promising views about moral reasoning and their related views about inner and outer realms. For a study of women in traditional China that both appreciates the richness and complexity of their lives but also makes clear the ways in which they suffered gender discrimination, see Dorothy Ko, *Teachers of the Inner Chambers: Women and Culture in Seventeenth-Century China* (Stanford, CA: Stanford University Press, 1994).

15. Traditional Confucians do make the important point that the public realm calls for virtues such as "concern for the common good" (*gong* 公) that have no clear correlates within the family. For this point, see Joseph Chan, "Exploring the Non-familial in Confucian Political Philosophy," in *The Politics of Affective Relations: East Asia and Beyond*, ed. Hahm Chaihark and Daniel A. Bell (New York: Lexington Books, 2004): 61–74. Compare the notion of "The world is for everyone," discussed in chapter 6.

16. The most important exception to this generalization is John Rawls's *A Theory of Justice*, though his account would be significantly strengthened by incorporating the insights of Confucianism. For a sketch of how this might be done, see the works by Erin M. Cline, "Two Senses of Justice: Confucianism, Rawls, and Comparative Political Philosophy" and *Confucius, Rawls, and the Sense of Justice*.

17. This is not to say that a range of thinkers, in the West as well as the East, did not explore this theme. For example, Mary Wollstonecraft, Jean-Jacques Rousseau, John Stuart Mill, as well as a number of contemporary Western thinkers, do so. What is special and characteristic about Confucians is the nature of their views and the emphasis they place upon the contributions of the family.

18. Piaget also argued that this is the origin of our most basic moral sensibilities. See Jean Piaget, *Play, Dreams, and Imitation in Childhood* (London: Routledge and Kegan Paul, 1972).

19. The special sense of moral autonomy I have in mind here is characteristic of Kantian moral theory. For an historical account of this special sense of moral autonomy, see Jerome B. Schneewind, *The Invention of Autonomy: A History of Modern Moral Philosophy* (Cambridge: Cambridge University Press, 1997). For a clear example of this kind of view,

see Joel Feinberg, "The Nature and Value of Rights," *Journal of Value Inquiry* 4.4 (1970): 243–60. One notable exception to the generalization made here is Harry G. Frankfurt. See for example his "Autonomy, Necessity, and Love," in *Necessity, Volition, and Love* (Cambridge, England: Cambridge University Press, 1999): 129–41.

20. Zhu Xi offers this explanation of *zhi* in his commentary on *Mengzi* 2A2 in his "*Collected Commentaries on the Mengzi*" (*Mengzi ji zhu* 孟子集注).

21. Such a general conception of the nature and role of ideal rulers still has considerable play not only in regard to East Asian governmental leaders but as a model for business leaders as well. Such ideas are not wholly unknown in the west. Our sense of Washington, Jefferson, Adams, Madison, as well as other early crafters of our political and social order as "Founding Fathers" has a great deal to do with our deep appreciation of how profoundly they cared for the people of our nation. This appellation is very much an expression of filial piety.

22. The method of "extending" (*tui* 推) moral feelings has been a central Confucian concern ever since Mengzi (391–308 BCE) first described this process. For a modern analysis of Mengzi's teaching, see my "Chinese Self Cultivation and Mengzi's Notion of Extension," in *Essays on Mencius' Moral Philosophy*, ed. Liu Xiusheng and Philip J. Ivanhoe (Indianapolis, IN: Hackett Publishing Company, 2002): 221–41.

23. Research in empirical psychology strongly supports this contention. While children show various moral inclinations, such as compassion and a sense of right and wrong, from very early ages, perhaps as early as three months old, justice *as fairness* is not part of their moral repertoire. Fairness is a sensibility that arises in older children, around eight years old, and generosity around nine or ten; these are the result of socialization. For an accessible introduction to this research, see the *60 Minutes* episode "Born good? Babies help unlock the origins of morality" on the Yale Infant Cognition Center (http://www.cbsnews.com/video/watch/?id=50135408n). These results strongly imply that, roughly speaking, Mengzi was right about the origin of virtues like compassion but Xunzi was correct about things like justice.

24. For an argument that social bonds preceded and served as the grounds for the development of language, see Mary Midgley, *The Solitary Self*.

25. For the idea that rights in general serve as a fallback, see Jeremy Waldron, "When Justice Replaces Affection: The Need for Rights," *Harvard Journal of Law and Public Policy* 11 (1988): 625–47. For an application of this idea to the Confucian tradition, see Joseph Chan, "A Confucian Perspective on Human Rights in China," in *The East Asian Challenge for Human Rights*, ed. J.R. Bauer and D.A. Bell (Cambridge: Cambridge University Press, 1999): 212–40.

Notes to Chapter 6

1. The twentieth-century Confucian philosopher Mou Zongsan 牟宗三 (1909–99), in works such as *The Way of Politics and the Way of Administration* (政道與治道) (Taibei: Xuesheng shuju, 1991) also criticized Confucianism's lack of theoretical justification for its political institutions. For a study which describes Mou's criticisms and then seeks to address some of these shortcomings by offering a modern Confucian justification for political authority, see chapter three of Stephen C. Angle, *Contemporary Confucian Political Philosophy: Toward a Progressive Confucianism* (Cambridge: Polity Press, 2012).

2. I explore this set of issues in greater detail in "Death and Dying in the *Analects*," in *Mortality in Traditional China*, ed. Amy L. Olberding and Philip J. Ivanhoe (Albany: State University of New York Press, 2011): 137–51.

3. This regular hazard of utopian visions has been insightfully explored by Isaiah Berlin, see "The Pursuit of the Ideal" and "The Decline of Utopian Ideas in the West," both in *The Crooked Timber of Humanity* (New York: Alfred A. Knopf, 1991).

4. This inherent tension in regard to virtue was first made clear by David S. Nivison. See his "The Paradox of Virtue," in *The Ways of Confucianism: Investigations in Chinese Philosophy,* ed. Bryan W. Van Nordern (La Salle, IL: Open Court, 1996): 31–43.

5. Contemporary Confucians have sought to fill in this lacuna in the tradition by developing a range of different political and social theories based upon and inspired by classical writings. Prominent among such thinkers are Jiang Qing and Kang Xiaoguang 康晓光. In many ways, they, and especially Jiang, follow the example of the early Republication Era reformer Kang Youwei 康有爲 (1858–1927). For an excellent anthology of such efforts in English, see Daniel A. Bell and Hahm Chaibong, *Confucianism for the Modern World* (New York: Cambridge University Press, 2003). See also works such as Joseph Chan, "Moral Autonomy, Civil Liberties, and Confucianism," *Philosophy East and West* 52:3 (2002): 281–310; Justin Tiwald, "A Right of Rebellion in the *Mengzi*?," *Dao: A Journal of Comparative Philosophy* 7.3 (Fall 2008): 269–82; and Sungmoon Kim, "Self-Transformation and Civil Society: Lockean vs. Confucian," *Dao: A Journal of Comparative Philosophy* 8:4 (Winter 2009): 383–401. See also the recent translation and discussion of Jiang's work: Jiang Qing, *A Confucian Constitutional Order: How China's Ancient Past Can Shape Its Political Future*, ed. Daniel A. Bell and Ruiping Fan, trans. Edmund Ryden (Princeton, NJ: Princeton University Press, 2012).

6. For example, it accords well with the type of republication government described in works such as the *Federalist Papers*. In my opinion, the greatest contribution Confucianism can make to contemporary

political philosophy and practice concerns its teachings on how to inspire and cultivate good civil servants; I think it has relatively much less to contribute concerning the form, structure, and foundations of good government. Arguably, what I recommend has been its greatest contribution throughout history: finding ways to inspire and develop more humane bureaucrats to serve in the civil service and offset the worst tendencies of a series of absolute monarchs. Confucianism offers a powerful and much needed ethical and spiritual teaching for civil servants, who are responsible for developing and enforcing most of the regulations that govern life in contemporary industrialized societies.

7. Joel J. Kupperman has done more than any other contemporary philosopher to bring out this neglected but critical feature of attending to the everyday not only in Confucianism but other East and South Asian traditions as well. For representative examples of his treatment of this theme, see his *Character* (New York: Oxford University Press, 1991); *Learning from Asian Philosophy*, (New York: Oxford University Press, 1999); and *Theories of Human Nature*, (Indianapolis, IN: Hackett Publishing, 2010).

8. Important exceptions to this generalization about the modern Western ethical tradition are found in some versions of virtue ethics and in the ethics of belief. These, though, are minority views within contemporary ethical discourse and the latter does not usually include concern about the control and shaping of feelings.

9. This conception of how we might work to improve ourselves depends upon a view of human nature as possessing at least some resources for and tendencies toward the good, which is a characteristic feature of most Confucian thought. Such a view could not easily take hold or develop in a culture that regards human nature as fundamentally or incorrigibly corrupt.

10. These are the concluding words of Abraham Lincoln's first inaugural address.

11. These characters commonly are transliterated into English as Kung Fu and associated exclusively with the martial arts.

12. See *Analects* 2.4, cited in chapter two.

13. The passage is from Wang's *A Record for Practice*. See my *Ethics in the Confucian Tradition: The Thought of Mengzi and Wang Yangming*, p. 102, for more context, a complete reference, and analysis.

14. For a good introduction to this practice in the Japanese neo-Confucian tradition, see Rodney L. Taylor, *The Confucian Way of Contemplation: Okada Takehiko and the Tradition of Quiet-Sitting* (Columbia: University of South Carolina Press, 1988).

15. There is a close correlation between early Confucianism and the kinds of "spiritual exercises" described by Pierre Hadot. See Pierre Hadot, *Philosophy as a Way of Life: Spiritual Exercises from Socrates to Foucault*, ed.

with an introduction by Arnold I. Davison, trans. by Michael Chase (Oxford: Blackwell, 1995).

16. In her recent brilliant study of virtue, Julia Annas argues for a much closer correlation between virtue and skill than most virtue ethicists allow. For example, she argues that "the need to learn" and "the drive to aspire" are shared characteristics of both many skills and virtue. In these respects, as well as others, her analysis resonates well with and helps us understand the Confucian tradition. See Julia Annas, *Intelligent Virtue* (New York: Oxford University Press, 2011).

17. The different moral dimensions of this song, both critical and exemplary, also illustrate some of the points raised and discussed in chapter four about the ethical potential of music.

18. Erin M. Cline makes a similar point in her insightful discussion of this passage in the context of discussing nameless virtues in the *Analects*. See her "Nameless Virtues and Restrained Speech in the Analects," *International Philosophical Quarterly* 49.143 (2009): 53–69.

19. A similar perspective on the natural world is beautifully presented by Annie Dillard; see her *Pilgrim at Tinker Creek* (New York: Harper Perennial Modern Classics, 1985).

20. Josiah Royce argues that most religions represent such "lost causes." See his *The Philosophy of Loyalty* (New York: Macmillan, 1908): 284–5. Kongzi did look back to a Golden Age and certain perfectly good sage-kings of ancient times as models, but these examples were all drawn from a quasi-mythic period of antiquity, and even the ideal Golden Age was destined to decline and fall apart.

21. The answers provided by the four disciples describe a spectrum moving from the direct and swift transformation of a state to an appreciation of the everyday. The first response, by Zilu, describes an aspiration and plan most removed from normal daily life and directly focused on social and political goals. Each successive answer to Kongzi's query brings us closer to more quotidian needs, concerns, and joys.

Note to Chapter 7

1. For a more complete translation and the reference, see my *Confucian Moral Self Cultivation,* p. 91.

WORKS CITED

Adams, Robert. "Saints." *The Journal of Philosophy* 81.7 (July 1984): 392–401.

Angle, Stephen C. *Contemporary Confucian Political Philosophy: Toward a Progressive Confucianism*. Cambridge: Polity Press, 2012.

Annas, Julia. *Intelligent Virtue*. New York: Oxford University Press, 2011.

Bai Tongdong. "A Mencian Version of Limited Democracy." *Res Publica* 14.1 (2008): 19–34.

Batson, C.D. "Prosocial Motivation: Is It Ever Truly Altruistic?" In *Advances in Experimental Social Psychology*, Volume 20, edited by L. Berkowitz. New York: Academic Press, 1987.

Bauer, J.R. and D.A. Bell, Eds. *The East Asian Challenge for Human Rights*. Cambridge: Cambridge University Press, 1999.

Bell, Daniel A. *China's New Confucianism: Politics and Everyday Life in a Changing Society*. Princeton, NJ: Princeton University Press, 2008.

———. *Beyond Liberal Democracy: Political Thinking for an East Asian Context*. Princeton, NJ: Princeton University Press, 2006.

Bell, Daniel A. and Hahm Chaibong, Eds. *Confucianism for the Modern World*. New York: Cambridge University Press, 2003.

Bellah, Robert, Richard Madsen, William M. Sullivan, Ann Swidler, and Steven M. Tipton. *The Good Society*. New York: Vintage Books, 1992.

———. *Habits of the Heart: Individualism and Commitment in American Life*. New York: Harper and Row, 1985.

Berlin, Isaiah. *The Crooked Timber of Humanity*. New York: Alfred A. Knopf, 1991.

Berthrong, John H. *All Under Heaven: Transforming Paradigms in Confucian-Christian Dialogue*. Albany: State University of New York Press, 1994.

Billioud, Sébastien and Joël Thoraval. "*Lijiao*: The Return of Ceremonies Honouring Confucius in Mainland China." *China Perspectives*, 4 (2009): 82–100.

Bloom, Allan. *The Closing of the American Mind*. New York: Simon & Schuster, 1987.

Blustein, Jeffrey. *Parents and Children: The Ethics of the Family*. New York: Oxford University Press, 1982.

Bol, Peter. *"This Culture of Ours": Intellectual Transitions in T'ang and Sung China*. Stanford, CA: Stanford University Press, 1992.

Brandom, Robert B. *Making It Explicit: Reasoning, Representing, and Discursive Commitment*. Cambridge, MA: Harvard University Press, 1994.

Brooks, Bruce E. and Taeko A. Brooks. *The Original Analects*. Revised Second Edition. New York: Columbia University Press, 2001.

Chan, Joseph. "Democracy and Meritocracy: Toward a Confucian Perspective." *Journal of Chinese Philosophy* 34.2 (2007): 179–93.

———. "Exploring the Non-familial in Confucian Political Philosophy." In *The Politics of Affective Relations: East Asia and Beyond*, edited by Hahm Chaihark and Daniel A. Bell. New York: Lexington Books, 2004.

———. "Moral Autonomy, Civil Liberties, and Confucianism." *Philosophy East and West* 52:3 (2002): 281–310.

———. "A Confucian Perspective on Human Rights in China." In *The East Asian Challenge for Human Rights*, edited by J.R. Bauer and D.A. Bell. Cambridge: Cambridge University Press, 1999.

Chan Sin Yee. "The Personal Is Political: Confucianism and Liberal Feminism," in *The Politics of Affective Relations*. Lanham, MD: Lexington, 2004.

Cheung, Joys H.Y. "'The North Wind Blows:' Sounding Bitterness in *The White-Haired Girl*, a Communist Political Ritual." In *Reading Chinese Music and Beyond*, edited by Joys H.Y. Cheung and King Chun Wong. Hong Kong: Chinese Civilization Centre, City University of Hong Kong, 2010.

Chin, Ann-ping. *Confucius: A Life of Thought and Politics*. New Haven, CT: Yale University Press, 2008.

Cline, Erin M. *Confucius, Rawls, and the Sense of Justice*. New York: Fordham University Press, 2013.

———. "Confucian Ethics, Public Policy, and the Nurse-Family Partnership." *Dao: A Journal of Comparative Philosophy* 11.3 (2012): 337–56.

———. "Two Senses of Justice: Confucianism, Rawls, and Comparative Political Philosophy." *Dao: A Journal of Comparative Philosophy* 6:4 (Winter 2007): 361–81.

———. "Nameless Virtues and Restrained Speech in the Analects." *International Philosophical Quarterly* 49.143 (2009): 53–69.

Cohen, Joshua. "Okin on Justice, Gender, and Family." *Canadian Journal of Philosophy* 22.2 (1992): 263–86.

Damasio, Antonio. *Descartes' Error: Emotion, Reason, and the Human Brain.* Revised Second Edition. New York: Penguin Books, 2005.

Darwall, Stephen. "The Invention of Autonomy." *European Journal of Philosophy* 7.3 (1999): 339–50.

de Waal, Frans. *The Age of Empathy: Nature's Lessons for a Kinder Society.* New York: Harmony Books, 2009.

Dillard, Annie. *Pilgrim at Tinker Creek.* New York: Harper Perennial Modern Classics, 1985.

Fan, Ruiping. *Reconstructionist Confucianism: Rethinking Morality after the West.* Dordrecht; New York: Springer, 2010.

Feinberg, Joel. "The Nature and Value of Rights." *Journal of Value Inquiry* 4.4 (1970): 243–60.

Fingarette, Herbert. *Confucius: The Secular as Sacred.* New York: Harper and Row, 1972.

Flanagan, Owen J. *Varieties of Moral Personality: Ethics and Psychological Realism.* Cambridge, MA: Harvard University Press, 1991.

———. "Moral Science? Still Metaphysical After All These Years." In *Personality, Identity and Character: Explorations in Moral psychology*, edited by Darcia Narvaez and Daniel K. Lapsley. New York: Cambridge University Press, 2009.

Fleischacker, Samuel. *The Ethics of Culture.* Ithaca and London: Cornell University Press, 1994.

Frankfurt, Harry G. "The Freedom of the Will and the Concept of a Person." *The Journal of Philosophy* 68.1 (1971): 5–20.

———. *Necessity, Volition, and Love.* Cambridge, England: Cambridge University Press, 1999.

Goffman, Erving. *The Presentation of Self in Everyday Life.* New York: Anchor Books, 1959.

Goldin, Paul. *Rituals of the Way.* LaSalle, IL: Open Court Press, 1999.

Grotius, Hugo. *The Laws of War and Peace.* Translated by Francis W. Kelsey. New York: Carnegie Endowment for International Peace, 1925.

Hadot, Pierre. *Philosophy as a Way of Life: Spiritual Exercises from Socrates to Foucault.* Edited with an Introduction by Arnold I. Davison. Translated by Michael Chase. Oxford: Blackwell, 1995.

Henderson, John. *Scripture, Canon, and Commentary.* Princeton, NJ: Princeton University Press, 1991.

Herder, Johann Gottfried. *Voices of the People in Their Songs (Stimmen der Völker in ihren Liedern)*, 1773.

Higgins, Kathleen M. "Music in Confucian and Neo-Confucian Philosophy." *International Philosophical Quarterly* 20.4 (1980): 433–51.

———. *The Music of Our Lives*. Philadelphia: Temple University Press, 1991.

Hoffman, Martin L. *Empathy and Moral Development: Implications for Caring and Justice*. Reprint. New York: Cambridge University Press, 2007.

Huang, Ch'un-chieh. *Mencian Hermeneutics: A History of Interpretations in China*. New Brunswick, NJ: Transaction Publishers, 2001.

Hutton, Eric L. *Virtue and Reason in Xunzi*. Ph.D. dissertation, Stanford University, 2001.

Ivanhoe, Philip J. "Senses and Values of Oneness." In *The Philosophical Challenge from China*, edited by Brian Bruya. Cambridge, MA: MIT Press, 2014.

———. "Happiness in Early Chinese Thought." In *Oxford Handbook of Happiness*, edited by Ilona Boniwell and Susan David. Oxford, England: Oxford University Press, 2011.

———. "Death and Dying in the *Analects*." In *Mortality in Traditional China*, edited by Amy L. Olberding and Philip J. Ivanhoe. Albany: State University of New York Press, 2011.

———. "Lessons from the Past: Zhang Xuecheng and the Ethical Dimensions of History." *Dao: A Journal of Comparative Philosophy* 8.2 (June, 2009): 189–203.

———. "Filial Piety as a Virtue." In *Working Virtue: Virtue Ethics and Contemporary Moral Problems*, edited by Rebecca Walker and Philip J. Ivanhoe. Oxford: Clarendon Press, 2007.

———. "Heaven as a Source for Ethical Warrant in Early Confucianism." *Dao: A Journal of Comparative Philosophy* 6.3 (2007): 211–20.

———. *Confucian Moral Self Cultivation*. Revised Second Edition. Indianapolis, IN: Hackett Publishing Company, 2006.

———. "Chinese Self Cultivation and Mengzi's Notion of Extension." In *Essays on Mencius' Moral Philosophy*, edited by Liu Xiusheng and Philip J. Ivanhoe. Indianapolis, IN: Hackett Publishing Company, 2002.

———. "The Concept of *De* ('Virtue') in the *Laozi*." In *Religious and Philosophical Aspects of the Laozi*, edited by Mark Csikszentmihalyi and Philip J. Ivanhoe. Albany: State University of New York Press, 1999.

———. *Ethics in the Confucian Tradition: The Thought of Mengzi and Wang Yangming*. Revised Second Edition. Indianapolis, IN: Hackett Publishing Company, 2002.

Jiang, Qing. *A Confucian Constitutional Order: How China's Ancient Past Can Shape Its Political Future*. Edited by Daniel A. Bell and Ruiping Fan. Trans. by Edmund Ryden. Princeton, NJ: Princeton University Press, 2012.

Kellert, Stephen R. and Edward O. Wilson, Eds. *The Biophilia Hypothesis*. Reprint. Washington, D.C.: Island Press, 1995.

Kierkegaard, Søren Aabye. *Sickness Unto Death*. Translated by Howard V. Hong and Edna H. Hong. Princeton, NJ: Princeton University Press, 1980.

Kim, Sungmoon. "Self-Transformation and Civil Society: Lockean vs. Confucian." *Dao: A Journal of Comparative Philosophy* 8:4 (Winter 2009): 383–401.

Kline, T.C. III. *Ethics and Tradition in the* Xunzi. Ph.D. dissertation. Stanford University, 1998.

Kline, T.C. III and Philip J. Ivanhoe, Eds. *Virtue, Nature and Agency in the Xunzi*. Indianapolis, IN: Hackett Publishing Company, 2000.

Ko, Dorothy. *Teachers of the Inner Chambers: Women and Culture in Seventeenth-Century China*. Stanford, CA: Stanford University Press, 1994.

Kralik, John. *365 Thank Yous: The Year a Simple Act of Daily Gratitude Changed My Life*. New York: Hyperion Books, 2010.

Kupperman, Joel J. *Character*. New York: Oxford University Press, 1991.

———. *Learning from Asian Philosophy*. New York: Oxford University Press, 1999.

———. "Naturalness Revisited: Why Western Philosophers Should Study Confucius." In *Confucius and the Analects: New Essays*, edited by Bryan W. Van Norden. New York: Oxford University Press, 2002.

———. *Theories of Human Nature*. Indianapolis, IN: Hackett Publishing, 2010.

Langer, Susanne K. *Philosophy in a New Key: A Study in the Symbolism of Reason, Rite, and Art*. New York: New American Library, 1951.

Lee, Pauline Chen. "Li Zhi and John Stuart Mill: A Confucian Feminist Critique of Liberal Feminism." In *The Sage and the Second Sex: Confucianism, Ethics, and Gender*, edited by Li Chenyang. Chicago: Open Court Press, 2000.

Levenson, Joseph R. *Confucian China and Its Modern Fate: A Trilogy*. Berkeley: University of California Press, 1965.

Li Chenyang. "The Confucian Concept of Jen and the Feminist Ethics of Care: A Comparative Study." *Hypatia: A Journal of Feminist Philosophy* (January 1994): 70–89.

Liu Xiusheng and Philip J. Ivanhoe, Eds. *Essays on the Moral Philosophy of Mengzi*. Indianapolis, IN: Hackett Publishing, 2002.

Loewe, Michael and Edward L. Shaughnessy, Eds. *The Cambridge History of Ancient China: From the Origins of Civilization to 221B.C.* New York: Cambridge University Press, 1999.

Louie, Kam. *Critiques of Confucius in Contemporary China.* Hong Kong: Chinese University Press, 1980.

MacIntyre, Alasdair. *After Virtue.* Second Edition. Notre Dame, IN: University of Notre Dame Press, 1984.

———. *Whose Justice? Which Rationality?* Notre Dame, IN: University of Notre Dame Press, 1988.

———. *Three Rival Versions of Moral Enquiry: Encyclopedia, Genealogy, and Tradition.* Notre Dame, IN: University of Notre Dame Press, 1990.

———. *Dependent Rational Animals: Why Human Beings Need the Virtues.* Chicago: Open Court, 1999.

Makeham, John. *Transmitters and Creators: Chinese Commentators and Commentaries on the Analects.* Harvard East Asian Monographs. Cambridge, MA: Harvard University Asia Center, 2004.

Marsalis, Wynton and Selwyn Seyfu Hinds. *To a Young Jazz Musician: Letters from the Road.* New York: Random House, 2004.

Midgley, Mary. *The Solitary Self: Darwin and the Selfish Gene.* Durham, England: Acumen, 2010.

Morgan, William J., ed. *Ethics in Sport.* Second Edition. Champaign, IL: Human Kinetics, 2007.

Mou Zongsan (牟宗三). *The Way of Politics and the Way of Administration* (政道與治道). Taibei: Xuesheng shuju, 1991.

Murphy, Liam and Thomas Nagel. *The Myth of Ownership: Taxes and Justice.* New York: Oxford University Press, 2002.

Neville, Robert C. *Boston Confucianism Portable Tradition in the Late-Modern World.* Albany: State University of New York Press, 2000.

Nivison, David S. "The Paradox of Virtue." In *The Ways of Confucianism: Investigations in Chinese Philosophy*, edited by Bryan W. Van Nodern. La Salle, IL: Open Court, 1996.

Nylan, Michael and Thomas Wilson. *Lives of Confucius: Civilization's Greatest Sage through the Ages.* New York: Doubleday, 2010.

Okin, Susan Moller. *Justice, Gender, and the Family.* New York: Basic Books, 1989.

Olberding, Amy. "'Ascending the Hall': Style and Moral Improvement in the *Analects.*" *Philosophy East and West.* 59.4 (October 2009): 503–22.

Olberding, Amy and Philip J. Ivanhoe, Eds. *Mortality in Traditional China.* Albany: State University of New York Press, 2011.

Patemen, Carole. *The Disorder of Women: Democracy, Feminism, and Political Theory.* Cambridge: Polity Press, 1989.

Pelikan, Jaroslav. *The Vindication of Tradition: The 1983 Jefferson Lecture in the Humanities*. New Haven, CT: Yale University Press, 1989.

Piaget, Jean. *Play, Dreams, and Imitation in Childhood*. London: Routledge and Kegan Paul, 1972.

Pinker, Steven. *The Better Angels of Our Nature: Why Violence Has Declined*. New York: Viking Penguin, 2011.

Putnam, Hilary. "Meaning and Reference." *The Journal of Philosophy* 70.19 (1973): 699–711.

———. *Meaning and the Moral Sciences*. London: Routledge and Kegan Paul, 1978.

Randall, John Herman. *The Making of the Modern Mind: A Survey of the Intellectual Background of the Present Age*. Reprint. New York: Columbia University Press, 1976.

Raphals, Lisa. *Sharing the Light: Representations of Women and Virtue in Early China*. Albany: State University of New York Press, 1998.

Rawls, John. *A Theory of Justice*. Cambridge, MA: The Belknap Press, 1971.

Rorty, Richard. "Cosmopolitanism without Emancipation: A Response to Jean-Francois Lyotard," in Richard Rorty. *Objectivity, Relativism and Truth*. Cambridge: Cambridge University Press, 1991.

Rosenlee, Li Hsiang Lisa. *Confucianism and Women: A Philosophical Interpretation*. Albany: State University of New York Press, 2007.

Royce, Josiah. *The Philosophy of Loyalty*. New York: Macmillan, 1908.

Sartre, Jean-Paul. *Being and Nothingness: An Essay in Phenomenological Ontology*. Translated by Hazel E. Barnes. New York: Pocket Press, 1978.

Scheffler, Samuel. *Human Morality*. New York: Oxford University Press, 1992.

Schilbrack, Kevin, ed. *Thinking Through Rituals: Philosophical Perspectives*. New York: Routledge, 2004.

Schneewind, Jerome B. *The Invention of Autonomy: A History of Modern Moral Philosophy*. Cambridge: Cambridge University Press, 1997.

Schwitzgebel, Eric. "Human Nature and Moral Development in Mencius, Xunzi, Hobbes, and Rousseau." *History of Philosophy Quarterly* 24 (2007): 147–68.

Scruton, Roger. *The Aesthetics of Music*. New York: Oxford University Press, 1999.

Searle, John. *The Construction of Social Reality*. New York: The Free Press, 1995.

Sen, Amartya K. "Rational Fools: A Critique of the Behavioral Foundations of Economic Theory." *Philosophy and Public Affairs* 6.4 (1977): 317–44.

Shils, Edward. *Tradition*. Chicago: University of Chicago Press, 1981.

Shun, Kwong-loi. *Mencius and Early Chinese Thought*. Stanford, CA: Stanford University Press, 1997.

———. "*Jen and Li* in the Analects." In *Confucius and the* Analects*: New Essays*, edited by Bryan W. Van Norden. New York: Oxford University Press, 2001.

Sidgwick, Henry. *The Methods of Ethics*. Seventh Edition. Indianapolis, IN: Hackett Publishing Company, 1981.

Singer, Peter. "Famine, Affluence, and Morality." *Philosophy and Public Affairs* 1.3 (1972): 229–43.

Sober, Elliot and David Sloan Wilson. *Unto Others: The Evolution and Psychology of Unselfish Behavior*. Cambridge, MA: Harvard University Press, 1998.

Stocker, Michael. "The Schizophrenia of Modern Ethical Theories." In *Virtue Ethics*, edited by Roger Crisp and Michael Slote. New York: Oxford University Press, 1998.

Stout, Jeffrey. *Democracy and Tradition*. Princeton, NJ: Princeton University Press, 2004.

Taylor, Charles. *Sources of the Self: The Making of Modern Identity*. Cambridge, MA: Harvard University Press, 1989.

———. *Human Agency and Language: Philosophical Papers 1*. Cambridge: Cambridge University Press, 1990.

———. *The Ethics of Authenticity*. Cambridge, MA: Harvard University Press, 1991.

Taylor, Rodney L. *The Confucian Way of Contemplation: Okada Takehiko and the Tradition of Quiet-Sitting*. Columbia: University of South Carolina Press, 1988.

Thompson, William Forde. *Music, Thought, and Feeling: Understanding the Psychology of Music*. New York: Oxford University Press, 2008.

Tien, David W. "Oneness and Self-Centeredness in the Moral Psychology of Wang Yangming." *Journal of Religious Ethics* 40.1 (2012): 52–71.

Tiwald, Justin. "A Right of Rebellion in the *Mengzi*?" *Dao: A Journal of Comparative Philosophy* 7.3 (Fall 2008): 269–82.

Tiwald, Justin and T.C. Kline III, Eds. *Ritual and Religion in the Xunzi*. Albany: State University of New York Press, forthcoming.

Tu Weiming. *Centrality and Commonality: An Essay on Confucian Religiousness*. Albany: State University of New York Press, 1989.

Tu Weiming, ed. *The Living Tree: Changing Meaning of Being Chinese Today*. Palo Alto, CA: Stanford University Press, 1994.

Van Norden, Bryan W., ed. *The Ways of Confucianism: Investigations in Chinese Philosophy*. La Salle, IL: Open Court, 1996.

————. *Confucius and the Analects: New Essays*. New York: Oxford University Press, 2002.

Waldron, Jeremy. "When Justice Replaces Affection: The Need for Rights." *Harvard Journal of Law and Public Policy* 11 (1988): 625–47.

Walker, Rebecca and Philip J. Ivanhoe, Eds. *Working Virtue: Virtue Ethics and Contemporary Moral Problems*. New York: Oxford University Press, 2007.

Wang, Robin R., ed. *Images of Women in Chinese Thought and Culture: Writings from the Pre-Qin Period to the Song Dynasty*. Indianapolis, IN: Hackett Publishing Company, 2003.

Wilburn, Brad K. "Moral Self-Improvement." In *Moral Cultivation: Essays on the Development of Character and Virtue*, edited by Brad K. Wilburn. Lanham, MD: Lexington Books, 2007.

Wilson, Edwin O. *Biophilia*. Cambridge, MA: Harvard University Press, 1984.

Wilson, Stephen. "Conformity, Individuality and the Nature of Virtue: A Classical Confucian Contribution to Contemporary Ethical Reflection." In *Confucius and the* Analects: *New Essays*, edited by Bryan W. Van Norden. New York: Oxford University Press, 2001.

Wittgenstein, Ludwig. *Philosophical Investigations*. Translated by William H. Brenner. Albany: State University of New York Press, 1999.

Wolf, Susan. "Moral Saints." *The Journal of Philosophy* 79.8 (August, 1982): 419–39.

Yu Dan. *Confucius from the Heart: Ancient Wisdom for Today's World*. London: Macmillan, 2009.

SUGGESTED FURTHER READINGS

General Studies of Chinese Thought and Confucianism

Berthrong, John H. and Evelyn N. Berthrong. *Confucianism: A Short Introduction*. Oxford: Oneworld, 2000.

Creel, Herrlee G. *Confucius: The Man and the Myth*. New York: John Day Company, 1949.

Fung, Yu-lan. *A History of Chinese Philosophy*, Volumes I & II, Second Edition. Trans. by Derk Bodde. Princeton, NJ: Princeton University Press, 1982.

Graham, Angus C. *Disputers of the Tao: Philosophical Argument in Ancient China*. Chicago and La Salle, IL: Open Court Press, 1989.

Hall, David L. and Roger T. Ames. *Thinking Through Confucius*. Albany: State University of New York Press, 1987.

Kupperman, Joel J. *Learning from Asian Philosophy*. New York: Oxford University Press, 1999.

Munro, Donald J. *The Concept of Man in Early China*. Stanford, CA: Stanford University Press, 1969.

Nivison, David S. *The Ways of Confucianism: Investigations in Chinese Philosophy*. Edited by Bryan W. Van Norden. LaSalle, IL: Open Court Press, 1996.

Schwartz, Benjamin I. *The World of Thought in Ancient China*. Cambridge, MA: Harvard University Press, 1985.

Tu Weiming. *Humanity and Self-Cultivation*. Berkeley, CA: Asian Humanities Press, 1979.

Van Norden, Bryan W. *Introduction to Classical Chinese Philosophy*. Indianapolis, IN: Hackett Publishing Company, 2011.

Translations of the *Analects*

Ames, Roger T. and Henry Rosemont, Jr., trans. *The Analects of Confucius: A Philosophical Translation*. New York: Ballantine Books, 1999.

Lau, D.C., trans. *Confucius: The Analects*. New York: Dorset Press, 1979.

Leys, Simon, trans. *The Analects of Confucius*. New York: W.W. Norton and Company 1997.

Slingerland, Edward G. III, trans. *Confucius Analects with Selections from Traditional Commentaries*. Indianapolis, IN: Hackett Publishing Company, 2003.

Waley, Arthur, trans. *The Analects of Confucius*. New York: Vintage Books, 1938.

Watson, Burton, trans. *The Analects of Confucius*. New York: Columbia University Press, 2009.

INDEX